THE
ANXIETY
CURE

In the UK more than 11 million people have been diagnosed with anxiety disorders. Almost two million of them suffer from constantly recurring panic attacks. More than anything else, they would love to live a normal life again as soon as possible: a life free from fear of fear.

Many years ago, Klaus Bernhardt experienced first-hand how little help people with anxiety and panic disorders could expect from traditional therapies. Therefore, he decided to do everything in his power to help those affected as quickly and as thoroughly as possible. So he specialised in treating anxiety disorders at his Berlin psychotherapy clinic, and today he is one of the pioneering therapists in Germany applying an entirely new therapy methodology. Its roots lie in cutting-edge neuroscience and it has nothing in common with standard therapeutic practice. You won't see exposure therapy in Bernhardt's clinic, or breathing exercises, progressive muscle relaxation, or digging around in childhood memories.

He also strictly rejects tranquillisers and antidepressants in almost all cases. With success: currently, 70 per cent of his patients need fewer than six sessions to be completely cured of their panic attacks.

THE
ANXIETY
CURE

THE PROVEN PROGRAMME

live a life
free from panic

KLAUS
BERNHARDT

Vermilion
LONDON

1 3 5 7 9 10 8 6 4 2

Vermilion, an imprint of Ebury Publishing,
20 Vauxhall Bridge Road,
London SW1V 2SA

Vermilion is part of the Penguin Random House group of companies
whose addresses can be found at global.penguinrandomhouse.com

Penguin
Random House
UK

First published in the United Kingdom by Vermilion in 2018

www.penguin.co.uk

A CIP catalogue record for this book is available from
the British Library

ISBN 9781785041938

Typeset in 11.2 /16.6 pt Sabon LT Std
by Integra Software Services Pvt. Ltd, Pondicherry

Printed and bound in Great Britain by Clays Ltd, St Ives PLC

CONTENTS

CHAPTER 4: Rewiring your brain

CHAPTER 5: Dealing with emergencies: first aid in seconds

CHAPTER 6: Finally free from anxiety and panic attacks

PREFACE

In the UK, more than 11 million people have been diagnosed with anxiety disorders. Almost two million of them suffer from constantly recurring panic attacks. More than anything else, they would love to live a normal life again as soon as possible: a life free from fear of fear.

Many years ago my experiences in the field led me to decide to do everything in my power to help people suffering from panic attacks faster and more comprehensively than previously possible. In our Berlin clinic, where we specialise in the treatment of anxiety disorders, my wife and I use a completely new methodology for treating anxiety, one derived from modern neuroscience. Our methods have little in common with the usual treatments anxiety patients have come to expect. At our clinic there is no exposure therapy, no breathing exercises, no progressive muscle relaxation and no digging around in childhood memories. With very few exceptions we also strictly reject the use of antidepressants and tranquillisers. When we are asked just why our form of therapy is so radically different from that of most of our colleagues, I like to quote Albert Einstein: *'The definition of insanity is doing the same thing over and over and expecting different results.'*

Regrettably, this clever quote perfectly describes much of the manner in which anxiety patients are currently treated. The same therapies are turned to again and again, despite their painful slowness in producing results – if they even help at all. At the same time, it appears that ground-breaking developments in neuroscience are being ignored. Instead of taking these new findings on board to finally establish better therapeutic standards, antidepressants continue to be prescribed and methods are still being used that in many cases have barely evolved in decades. Yet in the last 20 years, our understanding of the brain and how it works has been transformed. Thanks to imaging technology we can watch our grey cells think. We can test which thoughts and mental exercises produce which reactions, and thanks to the Internet, experts can keep in contact and up to date worldwide.

Thanks to these developments, we now have a very good understanding of what has to happen in the brain to make panic attacks possible, and we also know what can be to done to stop anxiety in its tracks. All of the techniques described in this book have undergone years of testing and refinement in our clinic. You may find it hard to imagine, but we are now at a point where 70 per cent of our patients need fewer than six sessions to be completely freed of their panic attacks.

Of course, a book can and should never replace an experienced doctor or therapist. But this book can still help you understand what really causes your panic attacks. You will also get to know a series of exciting and simple to learn techniques that have already helped many of our patients to live a life free from anxiety and panic.

I sincerely hope that the following chapters will help you to achieve that life as quickly as possible.

Yours
Klaus Bernhardt

Science and medical journalist, registered alternative psychotherapist and member of the Academy for Neuroscientific Education Management AFNB

1

PANIC ATTACKS: WHAT CAUSES THEM?

nxiety in general – and that includes panic attacks – is, first of all, our body's perfectly healthy and appropriate reaction to danger. For fear has only one job: to protect us. For example, if a hungry lion were to leap out of the brush directly in front of you, your body would immediately start producing adrenaline, your heart rate would go through the roof and within milliseconds you would decide whether you were prepared to fight – ill-advised, perhaps, with a lion sizing up its dinner – or flee. This is a completely normal and necessary reaction, which ensures our survival.

But what happens when there is no lion waiting to pounce? When your heart starts racing seemingly for no reason at all, when you feel like you are losing control or even going crazy, when for no apparent reason you suffer symptoms including dizziness, numbness, shortness of breath and nausea?

What exactly is happening in your brain, and why is it reacting the way it is? Well, there are basically four different causes, and I will devote a chapter to each cause. You can help yourself to recover more quickly by reading these chapters without skipping any of them, because panic attacks often have more than just the one cause. Only once you know all the causes, and are able to use the appropriate technique to deal with each one, will you be able to take charge of your anxiety quickly and sustainably.

Here's a short overview of the four most common causes of panic attacks.

Ignoring the warning signs

If there is one thing that I have learned from my years of clinical work, it is that ignoring warning signs is usually what triggers the initial occurrence of panic attacks.

But what exactly are these warning signs? Mostly, it starts when you have ignored your gut for far too long. Gut instinct is the voice of your unconscious. And the more often you use your conscious brain to come up with yet another argument as to why you can't listen to your gut, the louder your discontented unconscious will make itself heard. With the help of an eclectic variety of warning signals, which can be both mental and physical in nature, your unconscious seeks to get you to change something about your life that has long since stopped doing you good.

The mental warning signs include sudden forgetfulness and difficulty concentrating, lack of motivation, exhaustion and feeling sad for no apparent reason. A panic attack, incidentally, is the final stage and hence the strongest of the mental warning signs.

Among the physical warning signs are stomach and digestion problems, sudden problems with vision, rashes and other skin disorders, involuntary muscle twitching (tics), as well as increased urinary frequency. Even slipped discs and shingles have been shown to be often psychosomatic in nature, and therefore count among these warning signs. How this all connects together, and what you can do about it to save your psyche all this unpleasantness, is dealt with in detail in Chapter 2.

Substances that can trigger panic attacks

Drugs

There are certain medicines that have been proven to trigger panic attacks. Alongside antipsychotics, which are prescribed, for example, to schizophrenia patients, the thyroid hormone thyroxine, which is used in cases of an underactive thyroid, is also a potential trigger. In particular, women who have been diagnosed with Hashimoto's thyroiditis can react to the wrong dose of synthetic thyroxine with panic attacks. In any case, it is certainly a good idea to check whether you are still taking the right dose as this can change over time or with lifestyle changes. Several of my patients have also had good experiences with switching their medication to natural thyroid hormone supplements taken from pigs. You will find more on this in Chapter 3.1. and also on our website www.better-life-with-hashimotos-disease.com, which my wife and I set up specially for Hashimoto's thyroiditis patients.

Panic attacks are, however, much more frequently triggered by recreational drugs than by prescription medication. Psychoactive drugs change brain function, altering mood, perception and behaviour. The active ingredient in cannabis, THC, can trigger anxiety, as can ecstasy (MDMA) and cocaine. Psilocybin too, the psychoactive substance in magic mushrooms, is high on the list of panic-triggering substances. All of these drugs have a massive impact on our body's neurotransmitter balance, and temporarily switch off certain of our brain's protective systems. The interesting thing about this is that in certain ways, this can even make our brain more productive: consider famous painters and writers who have created great work under the influence of drugs, for example the best-selling author Stephen King.

To visualise the protective filters in the brain that are switched off by the consumption of drugs, imagine removing the filter from a water supply. The water can flow a lot faster now, but dirt and particles in the water are free to flow through the entire system, potentially causing significant damage. Damage that might be inflicted on the brain, for example, includes the formation of the neuronal connections that trigger panic attacks. If this happens just once, the risk of panic attacks reoccurring rises massively each time you take drugs. If you suffered your first panic attack within 48 hours of consuming drugs, you should stop taking them immediately. Be aware that it makes no difference if this was the first time you took that drug, or you have had years of experience using it. Once your body has reacted to a substance with a panic attack, then this substance should be off-limits for you from now on. Even – in fact, especially – when you are feeling better again. You are especially at risk of triggering renewed panic attacks by using drugs, because your brain has already undergone and remembered this experience.

Did you know that over the course of their lives, most people will experience at least one or two situations that feel like panic attacks? Their intensity can vary widely and they also have an extremely wide variety of causes: an allergic reaction to an antibiotic, for example, or a temporary vitamin B_{12} deficiency. A temporarily underactive thyroid caused by dietary issues is another known trigger, as are food intolerances. Yet no sooner than we start suffering a lack of a particular vitamin or other nutrient, our body will as a rule solve the problem on its own. We get cravings for a particular foodstuff that contains large amounts of the missing substance, and the feeling of panic disappears as fast as it came.

For vegetarians and vegans who miss out on important sources of vitamin B_{12} because of their diets (liver, meat, milk and eggs, for example), I recommend taking vitamin B_{12} in the form of a dietary supplement should you ever suffer a panic attack.

Food

Foodstuffs that cause bloating, or gluten (a protein found in almost all cereal products) intolerance, can also lead to panic attacks. At fault here is 'Roemheld syndrome'. It is named after its discoverer, the internist

Ludwig von Roemheld, who made a significant discovery at the start of the twentieth century. He found out that many people suffering from bloating or wind also complained of symptoms common to anxiety patients: hot flushes, shortness of breath, heart palpitations, anxiety, dizziness, disturbed sleep and irregular heartbeat (also known as extrasystole).

But what is behind it all? In the compendium of clinical medicine, the phenomenon is described as follows: 'Due to accumulation of air in the gastrointestinal tract the diaphragm is pressed upward and can directly or indirectly place pressure on the heart. This can result in various heart complaints, including pain that resembles angina pectoris. In extreme cases this can lead to brief loss of consciousness.'[1]

If you suffer from bloating or wind, there exists a real possibility that you too 'just' have Roemheld syndrome. Fortunately, a test exists that can quickly establish whether or not this is the case, and there is also a whole series of tried and tested home remedies that you can make use of here. Especially in the initial stages of an anxiety disorder, when the anxiety still has not deeply anchored itself structurally in the brain, the rule of thumb with Roemheld syndrome is: no pressure on the diaphragm, no anxiety.

The simplest thing to do is, as was done in Shakespeare's day, burp and fart to your heart's content.

Trapped wind would then never get the chance to build up the amount of internal pressure necessary to trigger these unpleasant symptoms in the first place. However, as this method of anxiety reduction is unlikely to be well received by your family, colleagues and friends, I suggest you modify your diet. Start out by avoiding anything that gives you wind for 14 days. If you really are suffering from Roemheld syndrome, simply changing your diet will notably reduce your anxiety symptoms. You'll find further information and a list of foods that tend to cause bloating, as well as a second list of foods that tend not to, on our website (www.the-anxiety-cure.com).

As the list of everything you should not be eating in this situation is rather long, and a well-balanced diet is so important for quality of life, here are four tricks that can help you significantly reduce bloating, without taking drastic steps to alter your diet.

TRICK 1: AVOID GLUTEN

To start off with, avoid anything containing gluten for a week. This means everything produced using cereals such as wheat, rye, spelt, oats or barley.

The fact is, many people suffer from an undiagnosed gluten intolerance. One reason for this is that blood tests only demonstrate whether you produce antibodies against gluten, and don't reveal anything else about how your body and brain react to the protein.

Fortunately, there is a simple way you can test this yourself. For a couple of days, make sure to keep track of whether and how quickly you start to feel tired after eating, and whether your concentration suffers. How well are you able to concentrate, for example, on days you only eat vegetables and perhaps a little meat or fish, compared to days you eat plenty of gluten? For my part, I notice a massive difference. I love fresh bread, but the days I eat it I find myself much less productive and able to concentrate than on days I avoid foodstuffs that contain gluten. Not to mention that my digestive system has a much easier time of it the days I go without.

TRICK 2: EAT FOODS WITH THE HIGHEST WATER CONTENT FIRST

Eat individual foodstuffs in the correct order and if possible separately from each other – and take a small break between each course.

Eating in the correct order means eating foods with the highest water content first! So don't enjoy fruit as dessert, but as an appetiser instead. Then treat yourself to a short break, and only then should you eat the foods containing a lot of protein and fat. You will find that this greatly reduces your problems with bloating.

Let's take a juicy piece of honeydew melon, for example, wrapped in Parma ham. Personally, I love this combination, but for many people it guarantees stomach troubles and bloating. Why? If you ate the melon on its own, it would pass through the stomach to the intestines within 30 minutes. But if you eat it with the ham, the melon needs much longer to digest, starts fermenting in the stomach, and the gases this produces press the diaphragm upward. In susceptible people this induces Roemheld syndrome together with its unpleasant side-effects.

TRICK 3: SUPPLEMENT YOUR DIET WITH CARAWAY AND GINGER

Sprinkle caraway seeds as a condiment on to your food, and try taking a teaspoon of freshly grated ginger before eating – both significantly reduce susceptibility to bloating. If you find raw ginger too spicy, ginger tea is a good alternative. Fennel tea, as well as tea made from a mixture of aniseed, fennel and caraway, effectively counteracts gas.

TRICK 4: GO FOR A WALK

Exercise, or at least go for a walk regularly. This strengthens the musculature of the diaphragm, and the stronger the diaphragm is, the harder it is for gases in the digestive tract to exert pressure on your heart.

Ideally, of course, you can combine all four of these tricks, in which case you will only have to avoid a handful of really gassy foods such as beans, leeks and some sweeteners. As a reward, you will find yourself fighting fatigue much less often, and who knows, perhaps getting a little more exercise combined with some new eating habits will be enough on its own to free you from panic attacks.

The dramatic impact of negative thinking on the brain

After a single panic attack, many people start fretting about what is wrong with them. Maybe something is wrong with their heart, or they have a brain tumour, or some other terrible illness. Terrified, they head to A&E to get themselves checked out. Usually, they are sent home after being told that it was 'just' a panic attack, and physically there is indeed nothing wrong with them.

For most people that is hard to believe; after all there is obviously something not right. So the worry continues. Further visits to the doctor are undertaken, in the hope that further check-ups will finally find the 'cause' of the attack.

Yet it is this pattern of behaviour itself that can lead a one-off event to develop into regular panic attacks. The combination of regular worrying with strong negative emotion has been shown to alter the structure of the brain. Within weeks or even days, fear of fear turns into a completely automated pattern of thought that deeply roots itself in the synaptic connections of the brain. How is this possible?

When you think something, you are able to remember the thought afterwards. So it must somehow have been stored in your brain. But of course we don't have a hard drive in our head to write data to, as would happen with a computer. Instead, we save our thoughts biologically, in the form of synapses. Every single one of your thoughts creates neuronal connections in your head, even in the very moment you think that thought. In 2000, this discovery was honoured with the Nobel Prize in Medicine and has made a significant contribution in the development of new and more effective methods to combat anxiety. The scientist who we can thank for this discovery is Professor Eric Kandel, one of the most significant neuroscientists of our time.

Professor Kandel[2] conclusively demonstrated that all the thoughts we have and impressions we receive are stored in our brain in the form of synaptic connections. The stronger the emotions that underlie these thoughts, whether positive or negative, the more efficient the neuronal networks in our head. Therefore, one might say that repeated negative thinking builds the neurobiological foundation that allows panic attacks to happen in the first place. Anyone who thinks negatively for long enough is automatically laying down an information superhighway in their brain that travels directly toward negative feelings and anxiety. The route to joy and ease, on the other hand, is often reduced to a potholed lane.

Patients often ask me why their anxiety so often surfaces when they should be relaxing. Sitting on the sofa in the evening, on holiday, or even during a routine task like a long, boring drive on the motorway. The answer is simple: the human brain reacts not just to stress, but to periods of quiet too, depending on how it has been wired. What makes things more difficult is that our brain always wants to have something to do. As long as we have to fully concentrate on something, a telephone call, for example, a tricky chore, or just a pressing deadline, then our conscious brain has enough to do and we are largely free of anxiety and worry. However, as soon as calm returns, we become caught up in our thoughts again. Our brain tries to find something to do as quickly as possible. And where is it likely to find it most quickly – via that multi-lane information superhighway of negative thinking and anxiety, or the crumbling lane of joy and ease? Correct: from the information superhighway. In that moment, thanks to its established networks, it really is much easier for your brain to generate anxiety than a feeling of relaxation.

The way you think is constantly rewiring your brain. Every day, hundreds of thousands of connections are made in your brain, which stores everything that you have thought. Thoughts that repeatedly come to mind become ever more prominent, while neuronal access to thoughts that you have not paid attention to for a long time is dismantled. This is also the reason why you might struggle to recall the mathematical formulae you learned in school. If you did not actively think about it, direct neuronal access became lost. The very same thing has happened to your positive thoughts.

Our brain reacts completely automatically based on the way it is wired and used. That is, it adapts biologically to how you use it. Automatic processes are generated and, at some point, they control your brain, not you. This state of affairs is particularly insidious when it comes to pessimism. Instead of safeguarding you from disappointments, your brain is drilled to perceive more negatives than positives. Or to put it another way: you become blind to the beauty that surrounds you in the truest sense of the word, as well as all the possibilities open to you to make your life more enjoyable. I will explain again in more detail in Chapter 4 what exactly is happening in your brain.

Whether it was certain experiences you may have made that are responsible for you focusing solely on negatives and problems, or whether it is a pattern of behaviour you learned from your parents, is irrelevant to your recovery. The sole thing that matters is that you start building the right neuronal pathways in your brain, starting with a few simple tricks. That will take a little practice, of course, but the effort is more than worth it! As soon as you have learned all the techniques described in this book and chosen the ones that are right for you, you can start at once and reprogramme your brain for a life full of joy and without anxiety or panic attacks.

Right now, that might still sound like an impossible dream, but of course it is not, because the brain automates everything that you do regularly. That goes for cleaning your teeth, driving and touch-typing just as much it does for worrying and planning panic attacks. If you drive a car regularly, you will know what I mean. An experienced driver no longer needs to consciously think how to operate the clutch, when to change gear, or when to look in the rear-view mirror. These things will have a beginner breaking out in sweat, but an experienced driver does it all automatically and completely subconsciously. They can turn their attention to other things while driving, pursue a chain of thought, for example, listen to the radio, or have a lively discussion with a passenger. The reason for this is that our brain is permanently working to take as much of the load as it can off our conscious mind. As soon as our brain has recognised that a pattern exists, repetitive movement patterns, or thoughts, are moved from the cerebrum, the thinking part of the brain, to the cerebellum, where automated actions are stored. There, they are implemented automatically by the unconscious, leaving our conscious mind with as much free working memory as possible for new, unfamiliar tasks.

If you have had more negative than positive thoughts for many years and find it almost impossible to stop worrying all the time, you probably find it hard to believe that it really is possible to put a stop to the automated nature of negative thinking and hence all forms of anxiety disorder. And indeed, in the United Kingdom you would be hard pressed to find one of the standard forms of therapy as capable of having such a quick and lasting influence on the brain as the techniques presented in this book. Exposure therapy, digging around in childhood memories (psychoanalysis), breathing exercises or muscle relaxation do little to counteract negative synaptic development in the brain. In fact, the first two reinforce what urgently needs to be removed. Why this is the case is something I will tackle in detail in Chapter 4.2. Antidepressants and tranquillisers are incapable of effecting real structural change in the brain. At best, they can dampen the sensation of anxiety, not cure it. By the way, prescribing antidepressants for anxiety is common practice. Personally, with very few exceptions, I advise against it. For more on this topic, see Chapter 3.3.1..

A truly successful therapeutic method must ensure that, as quickly as possible, synapses that engrain a positive mental attitude are formed in the brain. As soon as enough of these connections are present, the brain starts to network this new information in the cerebellum of its own accord, setting up new automatisms that have a noticeable influence on your emotional world.

The latest findings in neuroscience enabled me to develop a special mental training routine that allows this very process to take place, multiple times faster than usual thought processes. You will start noticing the first changes after just a few days, and after three to six weeks the positive changes are impossible to ignore. In six to 12 weeks, 82 per cent of the patients under my personal care have managed to completely do away with their fear of fear, and hence their panic attacks too. In Chapters 4 and 5 you will get to know all the variations of this mental training system. I can imagine that you have half a mind to skip straight to this part of the book, but please be patient. In order for the process to work optimally, it is important for you to read and internalise the preceding chapters first. Only then is a fast and lasting recovery possible.

Secondary gain – when panic attacks have hidden benefits

Sometimes, my patients rid themselves of their panic attacks very quickly, only to be hit by a panic attack again a couple of weeks or months later. In many cases, 'secondary gain' is responsible. This describes a situation in which a patient is suffering from their anxiety disorder, but is also deriving some kind of hidden benefit from it, something they themselves are usually not consciously aware of. For example, their partner might have started being more attentive and considerate because of the panic attacks. Or perhaps the anxiety disorder serves as a legitimate excuse to stop going to a job that has long since ceased to be fulfilling. Perhaps someone has been caring for a sick relative for years, and the only way they can escape the obligation is to become ill themselves. The list of potential secondary gains is long. Most of those affected have an unusually strong sense of duty, and something 'really bad' has to happen before people aren't going to be able to count on them. In these cases, an anxiety disorder is often the only way some people can find to get out of obligations that they are no longer willing or able to do.

You probably find this hard to imagine, but I see these cases in my clinic on a regular basis. Panic attacks disappear just like that, from one day to the next, and only because the sufferer finally had the courage to look for a better job, for example, or engage a carer for an elderly parent. There are many potential variations for cases of secondary gain. I experienced a particularly interesting case a while ago in my clinic.

A case study of secondary gain

In February 2015, a lady sought me out at my clinic who had been suffering panic attacks for many years when travelling by car. Driving through long tunnels was especially difficult. The problem had become so severe that family holidays were planned to guarantee that there would be no tunnels along the route. The panic attacks of this 32-year-old, physically healthy woman determined where the family might go on holiday, which her husband and two children resented.

When she first visited my clinic in Berlin she already had two years of therapy behind her. However, the anxiety had not gone away, despite taking antidepressants on her doctor's advice for the last year and a half.

It took us four sessions, with the help of the Pitching Technique (see Chapter 5.6.2.), which I will return to later, to have her panic attacks vanish completely. She was able to gradually reduce the medication under the supervision of her GP, 'tapering', in medical jargon, until she was able to give it up completely after a few weeks. Driving became perfectly normal for her again, and even long tunnels were no challenge at all.

About eight months after this wonderful achievement, she called me completely distraught, telling me through tears that the panic attacks had suddenly come back and she had no idea why. So I invited her back to the clinic. I soon discovered that now she was able to drive anywhere she wanted again, a visit to her parents-in-law was long overdue. She had been spared that experience for almost three years, because her in-laws' home could only be reached by driving through a long tunnel. As a diagnosed anxiety patient, it was sadly no longer possible for her to drive there. Now, however, a date had been set and there was no way around it. My patient and her mother-in-law had a very fractious relationship, and previous visits had stressed her out so much they always resulted in her falling ill for a week afterwards. It was very clear that the panic attacks, along with the stress on a secondary level, protected my patient from having to deal with her mother-in law. This is why this psychodynamic phenomenon is called secondary gain. Illness serves to avoid something else, something unpleasant. Of course, this all takes place completely subconsciously. My patient hadn't faked her anxiety, after all; she had real panic attacks that she experienced, as so many others do, as genuinely life-threatening. And yet she also profited from the recurring panic attacks, because they saved her from going to see the 'wicked' mother-in-law.

I could tell from her reaction to my diagnosis that I had hit the nail on the head. It was quite clear that she needed to communicate to her family that she might be healthy again, but she still was not going to see the in-laws in the foreseeable future. She sat her husband down, and told him that going to her in-laws' place was a source of great anxiety for her, and together they decided that she would stay home whenever he took their children to visit his parents. Once she and her husband had agreed to this plan, the panic attacks instantly disappeared again.

So if you are suffering from panic attacks or other forms of anxiety, it is worth asking yourself the following questions: along with all the unpleasantness, is there also a positive side? What are you avoiding – a visit, a work task, or a change perhaps, something long overdue that you have not been able to gather the strength to under-take? Perhaps splitting from a partner, changing jobs, or moving? Frequently, my patients will refuse to accept the connection at first, because the fear of change appears bigger than the problem with the panic attacks. Yet here too, a well-trained therapist will be able to provide the necessary support to make these changes possible and help the patient enjoy a better quality of life as quickly and, most importantly, as sustainably as possible.

You still might find this hard to believe right now, but the fact remains: panic attacks are a completely normal and healthy protective reflex of your unconscious to shield you from something else – usually something worse. With the help of this book you can discover why your psyche has activated this emergency programme and what your options are to restore the normal state of affairs.

Summary: discovering the real causes of your anxiety

- Panic attacks are often warning signs, coming after you repeatedly ignored what your gut was telling you.
- Panic attacks can be triggered by drugs or the wrong medication.
- In some cases, panic attacks can be traced to undiagnosed Roemheld syndrome, which can only be completely cured with changed eating habits and a little more exercise.

- Panic attacks are often the result of habitual negative thought processes. With the right methods, these 'grooves' in the brain can be reversed.
- Sometimes, panic attacks can be a way of avoiding long-overdue change. As soon the situation does change, the anxiety disappears on its own.

2

RECOGNISING AND REACTING
TO THE WARNING SIGNS

Psychosomatic disturbances are often actually alarm bells set off by our unconscious to alert the conscious mind. It is therefore very important for your recovery to understand how your psyche manages to pull off the trick of causing real physical symptoms even though the body parts and organs affected are completely healthy. Since this is often never made clear in mainstream medicine, many people are legitimately frightened of being 'mentally ill', desperate that someone find a 'real' physical cause for their outbreak of panic attacks. Tingling arms and legs, numbness, a racing heart, stomach cramps, tightness in the chest and throat, dizziness, depersonalisation (the feeling of being a detached observer of oneself): they all feel so real that there *must* be some kind of physical cause. In a certain sense, there is, but in nearly all cases you are completely healthy both physically and mentally. Your psyche is simply trying to warn you that you need to alter certain behaviour or patterns of thinking, to avoid more serious damage in the long run. If in future you take heed of these warnings in time and react appropriately, you may well find your anxiety disorder and accompanying panic attacks soon disappear for ever.

The power of the unconscious

In order to better understand the processes at work inside you during a panic attack, let's look first of all at the brain, specifically the two completely different working methods of the conscious and unconscious mind.

An adult's brain contains around 86 billion nerve cells, also known as neurons. These are connected to each other by around 100 trillion synapses. That means that each individual brain cell is connected to at least 1,000 other brain cells. You might find it hard to picture, but the number of potential combinations of these neurons and their connections exceeds by far the number of grains of sand that exist on our beautiful planet. Remember, we are talking here about the possible combinations in a single human brain!

Our conscious mind, however, uses relatively little of this incredible capacity. It can perceive a maximum of eight pieces of information per second, and requires an average of three seconds to produce a fully formed thought. It used to be widely believed that we use just 10 per cent of our brain. Today of course we know that is not the case, for our unconscious makes full use of our grey cells' processing power. According to the latest research, it processes at least 80,000 pieces of information per second, making it 10,000 times faster (one might also say cleverer) than the conscious mind we are so proud of.

Panic attacks: the psyche's labour of love

So the real guiding force in our head is, and will continue to be, the unconscious. And this force communicates with us, with the help of our so-called gut instinct. I am sure you know what I mean by 'gut instinct': you are thinking something over, struggling to make a decision, weighing up the arguments, the pros and cons. But then there is that feeling in your belly. You have no basis for that feeling, simply a 'better not' or 'yeah, why not?' This feeling is known as your gut instinct, and it's a result of your unconscious using its immense processing power to gather all the pertinent data and compare it with all the data and experiences from your entire lifetime. This involves taking unbelievable numbers of data points into account that you would never think of consciously, including body language, posture, tone of voice, choice of words, or smell – numerous studies have shown that when choosing a mate, our unconscious brain is capable of judging whether we could produce healthy children with a potential partner by their smell alone. All this happens within a few tenths of a second.

While your conscious mind would be hopelessly overtaxed by this flood of data, for your unconscious, this is child's play. It makes its decision almost instantly based on the data it analyses, then it shares its decision with you by talking to you through your gut.

The cleverest decision you can make is to listen to your gut. Because if you do not, sooner or later it will likely lead to unpleasant consequences. Our unconscious is almost like a supercomputer, constantly updating us with an analysis of our current situation via our gut and recommending actions to take or actions to avoid. This all happens for a single reason: to protect us from harm. Those who refuse to listen to their gut – permanently acting against their better judgement – will receive warning signals from their unconscious, small at first, and then, if necessary, the alarm bells ring. Everyone knows these serious warning signals: we also call them psychosomatic illnesses. You see, thanks to neurotransmitters our brain is able to trigger genuine physical symptoms within seconds, even though the organs affected are perfectly healthy. I will come back to this phenomenon in just a moment, but first I would like to illustrate how these psycho-somatic mechanisms work for you with the use of an analogy.

Imagine a mum watching her four-year-old son playing football. The little boy, with his lack of experience and limited perception of the world, represents the conscious mind. The mother, in contrast, with her decades of life experience, and her capacity to think ahead, is the unconscious. Imagine too that the little boy is completely focused on playing football; he keeps kicking the ball and running and kicking the ball and running, never noticing that he is running towards a busy road. The alert mother – the unconscious – realises at once and shouts: 'Stop! Stay where you are!' She shouts once, twice and maybe – very loud – a third time. If the boy still doesn't listen to his mother, she will quickly catch up to him and pull him away from the street, perhaps at the last moment. The boy will presumably be shocked, and have difficulty understanding why his mother is so angry and why she grabbed him.

And the same thing happened to you when you had a panic attack. Like the mother in our example, your concerned unconscious grabbed you, as it were, by the collar, after you continued to ignore your gut instinct, and by means of a panic attack forced you to rethink something in your life. What that might be is something I have already touched on in Chapter 1, and I will return to the subject in more detail later.

Protecting you as best it can and preventing you from potentially spending too long running in the wrong direction and getting hurt is one of your unconscious's most important tasks. This is why it sometimes takes drastic measures. In this sense, panic attacks are less an illness and more a labour of love by our unconscious to shield us from more serious damage.

Perhaps you can see now where all these shocking physical reactions are coming from, apparently out of a clear blue sky. If you don't listen to your gut, then your unconscious simply takes harder measures. With the help of neurotransmitters, it ensures that these unignorable physical symptoms force you to stop doing certain things or at least reconsider them.

Neurotransmitters: your psyche's busy handymen

Neurotransmitters are endogenous messenger substances, which our brain can use to induce virtually any physical response. There are several dozen neurotransmitters: the best known are adrenaline, noradrenaline, serotonin, dopamine, oxytocin and histamine. With every anxious thought, your brain stimulates the release of adrenaline from the adrenal glands. This neurotransmitter increases heart rate, which in turn means that an increased supply of oxygen and nutrients is transported quickly around the body. The arms and legs especially receive a plentiful supply, for in a fear-inducing situation it is important to be able to get away as quickly as possible, or at least defend yourself.

For people with an anxiety disorder, however, this surplus of oxygen and nutrients is not used for fight or flight: in fact, sufferers are often frozen by fear; some have difficulty even leaving the house. So the body needs to find another way to get rid of the surplus; after all, its overriding need is to return to a healthy balance as quickly as possible. It uses micro-movements of the muscles to make the process happen, which you may well be very familiar with: the tingling in your arms and legs as well as the sudden shivering that quickly drives up your body temperature to burn off the excess energy in the cells. Typical accompaniments are hot flushes and hands damp with sweat. These symptoms should therefore no longer be a source of worry for you. If this happens, it simply means your body is functioning perfectly and is only doing what is necessary to restore a state of balance.

If, however, a panic attack leaves you feeling cold rather than hot, then the likelihood is that the anxiety has led you to start breathing especially quickly and deeply. Hyperventilating in this manner ensures that more carbon dioxide is breathed out, driving up the pH value of your blood. This in turn alters certain metabolic processes in your body, and the blood supply to your hands, feet and brain rapidly worsens. Here, the result can often be dizziness, damp and tingling skin, and even muscle cramps.

In extreme cases, which are fortunately very rare, this can even cause you to faint, but even this is another protective mechanism put to work by your sophisticated and perfectly functioning body. It is in fact a tremendously efficient – if radical – method to ensure that you start breathing normally again. For that is what happens as soon as someone loses consciousness, even though these temporary blackouts usually last only a few seconds.

So please be aware that all the unpleasant physical symptoms that you might already have experienced had only one purpose: to protect you from suffering something worse. This even explains diarrhoea and stomach cramps. The neurotransmitter histamine is also released along with adrenaline. This governs skin response and also certain functions of the stomach, the intestines and the bronchial tubes. One of the effects of histamine is that during anxiety, the stomach suddenly cramps. This too is only happening to help us. Once anxious thoughts have put us in fight-or-flight mode, then of course our main concern is focusing all our energy on saving ourselves. So the brain uses histamine to slam the brakes on the digestive system; digestion is extremely energy-intensive, and in fear-inducing situations we need all systems prepared to either fight or flee.

Histamine also sees to it that any unnecessary ballast is thrown overboard. This ancient genetic programming may not serve any practical purpose for modern human beings, but seen in light of our developmental history it makes tremendous sense. If you have seen a nature documentary, you may know what I am referring to: animals running for their life expel urine and excrement. They relieve themselves in order to run away even faster, for even this small loss of weight boosts speed and could mean the difference between life and death.

We too carry these genetic roots within us. People who suffer from panic attacks often feel the need to urinate soon after the attack. This phenomenon is completely normal and is as old as mankind itself. Hence why it is also part of our language – think of someone who just watched a horror movie saying: 'I nearly wet myself.' If you think about it, there are many more expressions in everyday use that describe psychosomatic disturbances: 'It got under my skin', 'It took my breath away', 'I had a sinking feeling in my stomach', or 'It pulled the ground from beneath my feet'. All descriptions of physical reactions induced by different neurotransmitters, but without the body parts affected actually suffering from illness in any way.

However, if we force our unconscious to keep warning us in this way for too long, because fear of change makes us cling to things that are not doing us any good, then at some point even the healthiest body will start suffering the consequences. At this point, 'real' symptoms appear, although these will soon disappear again as soon as we have learned our lesson. Most stomach ulcers, slipped discs, chronic diarrhoea, cases of shingles and skin irritation can be traced back to this, and not a week goes by in my clinic without at least one patient quickly returning to health once they have learned to listen to the signals from their unconscious.

So spare yourself and your family all those visits to the doctor. That second gastroscopy or third heart exam is not going to give a different result. Instead, start listening to what your unconscious has been trying to tell you all this time, and to learn which techniques and exercises exist to get your brain – and your life – back on track.

The never-ending struggle: rational thought and gut instinct

Panic attacks are often nothing other than a labour of love by your unconscious, because fear of change has trapped you for far too long in a lifestyle that is quite simply making you ill. In your heart of hearts you might already have known that for a long time, but your conscious mind kept finding new reasons to put off those urgently needed changes. Then came the point where your unconscious had enough, and took drastic measures to make you start doing what you should have done a long time ago.

So it is about learning to listen to your gut again. But how can you tell whether something is coming from your unconscious, that is, decided by your gut, or instead has been decided by your head, that is, your rational brain? It is a lot simpler than you might think, because there is one very clear sign.

Your gut never argues, your brain always will.

When you gut says a firm 'no' to something, for example, when your boss asks you to do more overtime, your head usually starts making counter-arguments: 'Oh well, it's a good opportunity to make some extra cash.' 'Stop! You need a break.' But it does not give you reasons. The head, in contrast, will argue: 'Come on, you can do it, and by next week you can forget about it.'

But it is just when you have pushed yourself too hard that something usually goes wrong, and you spend the rest of the day fixing the mistake rather than doing anything productive. And as soon as you finally push yourself past your limits, your psyche will take matters into its own hands to ensure you get the downtime you need, as a rule by making you ill. It may still be hard to believe, but the fact remains:

> Your rational brain will never be as clever as your unconscious speaking to you via your gut instinct.

So my advice to you is: stop doing the opposite of what your gut tells you, because it has only one aim, to protect you as best it can and to prevent you from running in the wrong direction and getting hurt.

Admittedly, there is one caveat. Only those who have *suddenly* started suffering anxiety symptoms possess a healthy gut instinct in the first place. For example, someone who used to love driving before suddenly and unexpectedly having their first panic attack, and then for fear of suffering another one starts avoiding tunnels and motorways.

The situation is different for people who have always been anxious, perhaps having never taken their driving test due to anxiety. These people, in most cases because of their mirror neurons (neurons that make toddlers copy the behaviour of their parents), have learned to be excessively anxious since they were children and programmed their brains correspondingly. In many cases they also suffer from more or less intense social phobia. Here, it will usually take somewhat longer until they are finally free of anxiety and insecurity, because extremely old patterns of behaviour need to be unlearned and replaced with completely new ones. Still, if the techniques in this book are applied correctly and consistently, this process too should take no longer than four to six months, as my experiences with numerous patients in my clinic have shown.

The doctor says nothing is wrong

Now that you understand how the body can induce certain symptoms spontaneously, and perhaps have an understanding of why this is, it should be clear why no one was able to find anything physically wrong with you. There was nothing to find! You can be happy about that, because it means your problems can be solved using a few neuroscientific 'tricks' – which we shall come to in detail later – all much easier than medication or even operations.

Underestimating the power of the unconscious and treating psychosomatic illness as if there were genuine physical problems is, by the way, much more widespread than you might like to think. For example, many of my patients complain of high blood pressure. Some of them measure theirs several times a day, and more than one has been taking beta blockers for years to keep it under control.

Yet simple fear of high blood pressure is in itself enough to send it soaring. This phenomenon has seen extensive medical research, and it has its own name: white coat hypertension, or white coat syndrome.[3] It is called this because in many people, the mere sight of a doctor's coat is enough to send their blood pressure through the roof.

Something similar happens to people taking their own blood pressure at home and worrying about the result. My advice is to monitor blood pressure over 24 hours. If the results show that your blood pressure is generally at a healthy level, you should have a discussion with your doctor about gradually coming off beta blockers. For if you take medication you do not really need for years due to false measurements, your body can suffer significant damage. Sporadic phases of high blood pressure, spread throughout the day, are certainly no good reason to turn straight to powerful drugs.

I am sure you will already have noticed that it is important to me to try to explain to you as simply and clearly as possible what has been taking place in your body up till now. What I want is for you to take responsibility for your life again, instead of simply blindly relying on the pronouncements of doctors and therapists. Sometimes, a little common sense is all it takes to see that not every well-intentioned piece of advice is helpful.

Let me clarify that, using the example of high blood pressure again. Imagine that you have to water a garden. But your garden hose does not quite reach that far corner. What do you do? Personally, I would put my thumb over the end of the hose. This instantly increases the water pressure inside, and the water flows faster and sprays farther. Your body works in much the same way. As soon as you get stressed out, it knows that your entire organism requires more oxygen and nutrients. So it narrows your arteries to increase the blood pressure. Now your body is being provided with everything it needs, fast, and the waste products from cell metabolism are transported away faster as well. This is a perfectly normal and healthy reaction by your body. Once the stressful situation is past, blood pressure normalises again. If, however, you interfere with this process by artificially lowering your blood pressure with beta blockers, your body has to find another way to make the blood flow faster, for instance, making your heart beat faster.

Blood tests too are another form of snapshot. Did you know that you can significantly alter the levels of many substances in your blood in two minutes with just a simple exercise? This was discovered by the American social psychologist Amy Cuddy[4] together with her colleagues Dana Carney and Andy Yap. All you have to do is adopt a 'power pose'. Make yourself comfortable in your office chair, fold your arms behind your neck and plonk your feet on the desk. Hold this 'boss pose' for at least two minutes, or better five. During this time, your testosterone levels rise measurably, while the stress hormone cortisol is noticeably reduced. Your risk tolerance also increases significantly, something that can be of significant benefit to anxiety patients.

It is often the little things that can bring about that decisive change. Listening to your gut, adopting a powerful posture, refusing to be blindly swallow every hastily prescribed medication and seeing panic attacks not as an illness, but for what they really are – an act of love by a caring unconscious.

So that you too will soon be able to rhapsodise about your new life, in the rest of this book along with misunderstood warning signs we will take a closer look at the three other possible triggers for panic attacks. For it is only once you have ensured that you have uncovered everything that is contributing to your anxiety disorder that you will be on the fast road to a happy and relaxed life.

Summary: why you aren't ill, even if it feels that way

In one of his bits, the doctor and stand-up comedian Dr Eckart von Hirschhausen tells the story of the penguin in the desert. The luckless bird is standing on scorching desert sand, wilting in the heat, and seems to have absolutely no chance of doing anything to improve the situation on its own. Little short legs make it hard to hike away, and as a flightless bird it cannot use its wings to finally find, somewhere, anywhere, cool, refreshing water. Poor penguin. How on earth did it end up in the desert? It can never, will never feel happy here. But is it the penguin that has something wrong with it, or is it simply that its surroundings are unsuitable?

You know of course that there is nothing wrong with the penguin. It is not ill, it is just not in its element, water. So instead of spending weeks wondering how it got in the desert in the first place, or which medicines might help, the bird should ask itself a single question: how can I get to water as fast as possible?

You are not sick either, even if it feels that way sometimes. You are just in the wrong environment. Maybe in the wrong job, the wrong relationship, or maybe you have the wrong circle of friends. And as soon as you do understand what is wrong, and find your way back to your natural element, you too will feel fine again.

Now that we are at the end of the chapter, let's look back on everything you have already learned about potential causes of panic attacks.

- Most panic attacks are triggered by ignoring for too long what your gut is telling you.

- Gut instinct can be distinguished from the rational brain because it never argues. So if you find yourself weighing up whether or not to pursue a course of action, it means you are thinking consciously, and not using your unconscious' unbelievably clever and refined decision-making apparatus.

- Constant brooding and negative thinking rewires the brain bit by bit, finally leading to the development of anxiety disorders or depression. In the long run, pessimism can be hazardous to your health.

- Panic attacks can sometimes have physical causes too. However, physical causes are almost never to blame for a regular, recurring panic disorder – it is the anxiety caused by having an initial attack that is almost always responsible.

- The physical symptoms of an anxiety disorder are induced by neurotransmitters. You are neither mentally nor physically ill. Your psyche is simply using this method to tell you to change something in your life, urgently.

3

STOPPING ANXIETY DISORDERS TRIGGERED BY EXTERNAL INFLUENCES

There are many external influences that can trigger an anxiety disorder. Certain medications or drugs, an unhappy family or work environment, disruptions in our social circles, even developments in society or politics. We will take a look at all of these factors individually, for multiple factors often influence each other. The more clearly you know which of these factors apply to you, the easier it will be for you to free yourself of fear, step by step.

There is a whole series of substances that have been shown to be potential triggers for panic attacks. They include antidepressants, for example, which – absurdly – are still prescribed to supposedly get rid of the very thing they often cause. Antipsychotics are another class of drugs that can potentially trigger anxiety and panic, as can the prohormone thyroxine, which I will come to in detail in a moment.

Much more common than panic attacks triggered by prescription medication, however, are those caused by drugs. Drugs of all kinds act on our brains – that is the reason we take them in the first place. The drug alcohol, for example, is enjoyed by many for its mood-enhancing and inhibition-lowering effect, or for its power to numb, depending on how much is consumed. Contrary to popular opinion, however, alcohol is very rarely responsible for panic disorders developing. However, with a number of other drugs, the chance of developing panic attacks sooner or later is almost a certainty. Above all, the active ingredient THC contained in marijuana plays a significant role, as do ecstasy and cocaine. Magic mushrooms too, as well as many of the new synthetic drugs that are currently flooding the market, have been conclusively shown to be triggers for anxiety disorders.

As mentioned in Chapter 1.2., if your first panic attack happens within 48 hours of consuming drugs, you should stop taking them immediately. For your brain has not only had a specific experience with this psychoactive substance, it retains it in its neurons. Every further encounter with this drug reactivates and reinforces these synapses, making it ever more probable that the unpleasant experience will be repeated.

You should also apply this same sense of caution to medication that you suspect might have been the trigger for your first panic attacks. If this is the case, you should contact your GP and share your concerns with them. Ask them if it is possible to reduce or withdraw from the medication, or if there might be alternatives.

Whichever substance triggered your anxiety and panic, the consumption of this psychoactive substance has already left behind a network of negative connections in your brain. These neuronal networks do not just disappear if you do not consume a particular drug any more. Therefore, it is crucial not only to abstain from consuming harmful substances, but also to reverse these connections as well. Unfortunately, there is no direct way to do this – it requires taking a small diversion.

New neuronal pathways with positive information must now be proactively formed using a special form of mental training. As soon as these are stronger than the original, negative networks, your brain will prefer to take the new, positive route, and the old, negative ones will gradually fall apart. I will explain the precise neurobiological process in detail in Chapter 4, as well as the role that cellular renewal plays.

Alternative medications can save the day

People who have been diagnosed with hypothyroidism, and must therefore take the prohormone thyroxine for the rest of their lives, have an increased risk of developing an anxiety disorder. Luckily, however, there are alternative medications that can lower this risk. In some cases, it can be of benefit to take, in addition to thyroxine (T_4), the second important thyroid hormone, triiodothyronine (T_3). The next time you receive treatment for your thyroid condition, make sure that you have your T_3 levels checked in addition to your T_4 levels, because it is just as important for your well-being as the T_4 that is normally measured.

Another potential way to get rid of panic attacks that were originally linked to an underactive thyroid is to switch from synthetic thyroid hormones to natural ones derived from pigs. For many of my patients this move was a success. Since the natural product contains a significantly broader array of active ingredients than the synthetic hormone, switching to it can provide additional benefits along with a significantly reduced susceptibility to panic attacks: several of my patients reported enjoying better quality sleep, others that they could lose weight more easily and were much less prone to mood swings.

Defence mechanisms: nausea, hot flushes and dizziness

The human body is a miracle. It has at its disposal fantastically clever early warning and defence mechanisms and spends a lifetime protecting us from harm.

When we eat something we should not have, or take drugs that produce an adverse effect, it reacts promptly with nausea, dizziness or hot flushes. We need to vomit, and get diarrhoea, both of which help us to expel the damaging substances from the body as quickly as possible.

Yet although it is easy enough for most people to imagine that eating poorly, misuse of prescription medications or abuse of drugs can very quickly lead to unpleasant physical reactions, many people find it difficult to comprehend that our psyche can generate very similar symptoms to warn us that we have spent too long in the wrong job, the wrong relationship, or the wrong environment. Yet the biochemical processes at work could well be compared to a case of poisoning. Whether we are damaging our body with medication, drugs, or repeatedly ignoring our inner voice, the worse the potential danger, the more stridently it will attempt to put a stop to this behaviour, with every means at its disposal.

Guided by neurotransmitters and hormones, we react to all unhealthy contact, whether physical or psychological, with similar symptoms: nausea, stomach cramps, feelings of excess heat or cold, dizziness, pain, unpleasant physical sensations and tachycardia (elevated heartbeat). The sole difference is that the symptoms triggered by a physical problem usually come on gradually, and only become serious after being repeatedly ignored, while the alarm signal activated by a particular substance will usually make itself felt at once.

Psychiatric medication: more curse than blessing?

Antidepressants

Because symptoms triggered by a psychological problem are often particularly severe, many doctors and therapists believe that the only way to quickly bring relief to their patients is to restore their mental balance using chemical means. No surprise then that antidepressants are among the most frequently prescribed drugs worldwide.

The idea behind it is that people who suffer from depression or anxiety have too little serotonin and noradrenaline available in their brain. These neurotransmitters are responsible for our ability to feel joy and happiness. The purpose of antidepressants is to make more of these neurotransmitters available again. That is the theory. But what about in practice? I have seen a great number of patients in my clinic who have told me that during a stay in hospital they had been given up to five different antidepressants because none of them were having the desired effect. One patient described it as being like stumbling around in the fog, hoping to bump into the active ingredient that would finally provide some relief.

Statements like these cannot come as a surprise if one considers some of the newer studies on this topic. Jay Fournier[5] at the University of Pennsylvania analysed six different studies and conclusively demonstrated that only in the most severe cases of depression did antidepressants produce a measurable effect. If one considers the entire spectrum of patients treated with these medications, the conclusion that has to be drawn is that antidepressants have any kind of positive impact on only around a quarter of them, whereas around three-quarters see no improvement at all, although of course they still suffer the unpleasant side-effects.

The thing is, antidepressants do not tackle the root of the problem, the neuronal connections in your brain. Instead, they manipulate your neurotransmitter supplies in the hope that you will be less sensitive to whatever is troubling you. It's like having a car with a leak in the radiator. Instead of fixing the radiator, you refill it every day so that the engine does not break down. The leak gets bigger and bigger over time, and your radius of action gets smaller and smaller, because of course you have to keep stopping all the time to keep it topped up.

It is obviously smarter to fix the leak instead of just fiddling around with the symptoms – and the same applies to an anxiety disorder. Here, the smart course of action is to use the right exercises to structurally alter the brain, to stop the anxiety disorder where it began, namely your brain's automated thought processes. Medicating against anxiety is in principle no different to continually adding water to a leaking radiator. At best it is a way of putting off the necessary repair, but the problem is not solved.

Scepticism about antidepressants has also been increasing for years in the scientific community, where the medications' capacity to fulfil the promises made by the pharmaceutical industry has been called into question. Major American pharmaceutical companies have already been handed multi-billion-dollar fines for consciously spreading lies about the effectiveness of antidepressants and antipsychotics in their market-ing. The latter drugs are often prescribed to anxiety patients, even though their applicability was and is heftily disputed.

In the USA, since 2005 antidepressant packaging has been required to carry the warning that consumption, particularly by young patients, increases the risk of suicide. That such bold and important warnings are placed on cigarette packets but, in Germany at least, not on medication, remains an absolute mystery to me. Anyone who wants to find out more about the real risks of antidepressants is advised to check our website www.the-anxiety-cure.com for further information.

Tranquillisers (benzodiazepines)

Alongside antidepressants, tranquillisers with a high dependency risk – benzodiazepines – are a common part of the medication arsenal against anxiety disorders. Currently, there are around 20 of these substances on the market, of which I encounter diazepam and lorazepam most frequently in my work. These drugs provide fast relaxation and relief from anxiety, usually within 20 minutes, which risks becoming the go-to response, particularly with anxiety patients.

Unfortunately, regular consumption over the course of as little as two weeks can lead to physical dependency on these substances. If a dependency on benzodiazepines already exists, stopping the medication cold turkey can lead to extremely severe withdrawal symptoms. It is, of course, better to avoid taking them in the first place, or take them only in a real emergency. Benzodiazepines do no more than dull the anxiety, and like antidepressants, they do nothing to solve the problem. If one considers the long list of possible side-effects, I would contend that in most cases psychopharmaceuticals (prescription drugs to alter mood or behaviour) are more of a curse than a blessing for panic and anxiety patients. But there is something very important to mention at this juncture:

If you are currently taking psychiatric medication, please do not make the mistake of stopping on your own

It is quite possible that your body is already so accustomed to the medication that suddenly stopping could produce a severe reaction. Please withdraw from the medication only after consulting your doctor, and under their supervision gradually taper off by slowly and carefully reducing the dose over a long period of time. Ideally, you would start this process only after having successfully practised the exercises contained in this book for a number of weeks so that you feel strong and secure enough again to deal with the withdrawal.

The key to health: personal responsibility and self-respect

The key to health is within you, for you alone are responsible for your life. Only you – not society, doctors, or even your family – has the power to make those final choices of what to do and what not to do.

No one is forcing you to take substances that do not do you any good. No one can demand of you to stay in a job that makes you unhappier with every passing day. No one can force you to associate with people who do not give you the love and respect you deserve. No one forces you, except yourself!

Yet we are not laying the blame for your situation at your feet here. What I want to do instead is show you a way out of this insecurity and anxiety, to put a stop to your suffering once and for all. But you can only take this step into a life of freedom and comfort once you are ready to take full responsibility for your own life.

It is also necessary to put fear of change behind you, for it is this very fear that leaves so many people trapped in situations that they are no longer able to cope with. But it does not have to be this way. As you read this book you will learn new strategies that will make change not only easy, but also fun. One of these strategies is uncovering false beliefs, that is to say, recognising the lies we tell ourselves every day. I would like to tell you a little story here.

I once had a female patient from northern Germany. For the sake of simplicity, let's call her Angela. Angela had been working for a large property management company for years. To start off with, she and a colleague had been responsible for around 320 flats. After the colleague left the firm to have a baby, Angela was forced to take on her workload as well, without receiving the raise that should have reflected this change in circumstances. In the course of the nine years that she worked for the company, the number of flats she was responsible for rose to more than 500, and as before it was her responsibility to deal with all of the tenants' problems. Her boss refused to hire another staff member; after all, Angela had managed to do it all on her own up to now. In doing so he ignored the fact that it had become completely normal for her to take work home with her at the weekend, which was the only way she could keep up with her workload. Her marriage was suffering under the strain, and her relationship with her adult daughter and her few remaining friends was deteriorating, because in the little free time that was left to her she simply did not have the energy to maintain her social life.

When Angela, apparently out of nowhere, started having panic attacks, she realised that something would have to change, and came to see me at my Berlin clinic.

After she had thoroughly explained her situation to me, I asked her why, given the circumstances, she had not sought out a new job many years ago.

Quick as a flash she replied: 'That's not so easy, I'm 49 now, at this age you won't find a new job so quickly. Besides, the pay is good. With my qualifications I'll be lucky to earn as much somewhere else. And besides, there are plenty of young people out there who are desperate for a job and who will work for a lot less.'

In return, I asked Angela how she could be so certain of all this. Had she ever applied for a job somewhere else? She had not, of course, for she was convinced that her perception of the situation was correct. So I asked her to put herself in the position of a potential new employer, another property management company, for example. Who would she prefer to hire? A 49-year-old with heaps of experience who had managed to look after more than 500 flats on her own for years? Someone who had already developed the self-confidence and self-assurance necessary to cope with such a challenging job alone thanks to years of dealing with a diverse array of tenants and a huge variety of problems?

Or would she rather hire someone young and inexperienced, someone with a lack of the requisite business smarts? A 28-year-old trying to stand firm against a furious long-term tenant old enough to be her father? Someone looking to start a family and who might decide to leave at any time? Gradually, it dawned on Angela that her supposed disadvantages in the job market were actually massive advantages. That same week she sent off two speculative job applications to different property management firms, and both wanted to hire her on the spot. Since she was still securely in her original job, she was in a comfortable position to negotiate her remuneration with them, and three months later she started her new job. From then on, she was free of panic attacks. She was now responsible for 180 flats instead of 500, her salary was over €5,000 higher, she finally had her weekends to herself again and she even saved 15 minutes on her commute every day. What a fantastic result, and all because she was prepared to take a clear look at the truthfulness of her own obstructive thoughts for the first time. And sad to think about each and every month she lost, because she did not make the decision to change earlier.

I hear stories like this almost every day in my clinic. People convince themselves of things without questioning whether their assumptions correspond with reality. Studies of this phenomenon have shown that we lie to ourselves up to 70 times a day, namely through incorrect thoughts that we simply accept as they pop into our heads. Unfortunately, though, every one of these thoughts has its influence on our lives and our well-being.

For people who have been used to thinking this way since childhood, because this was the way things were done at home, it can be helpful to practise an exercise designed to reverse it. The bestselling American author Byron Katie described one such system very well in her book *Loving What Is*,[6] which I frequently recommend to my patients. Using the questions contained in it, and with a little practice, it is possible to expose all the lies great and small with which you make your daily life unnecessarily complicated. In addition, as time goes on you will start noticing – and be able to take advantage of – more and more opportunities. Soon you will be the proactive and self-confident master of your own destiny, and your brain will be freed of automated thought processes of unnecessary panic and anxiety.

So much for personal responsibility: what about self-confidence? Why would someone turn to drugs again and again to remove themselves from reality? Why do millions of people take medication every day just to make themselves feel 'normal', or simply in order to keep 'functioning'? Why do so many drown their sorrows evening after evening? Why do so many people numb themselves with consumer goods, when they must long since have realised that all the objects they surround themselves with have done nothing to prevent them from feeling empty and alone?

How is it possible that people can end up so lacking in self-esteem?

And what did the people who do have healthy self-esteem do differently? Certainly, early childhood experiences will have had an influence. However, a series of new studies has shown that we retain a high degree of influence on our patterns of behaviour – and therefore on our self-esteem – even at an advanced age.

It all starts with being honest with ourselves.

Are we happy with the life that we have built for ourselves over the years? Or are we past the point where things started going wrong? Have we been following a dream that proved itself a nightmare many years ago, one that we cannot admit to ourselves? Perhaps that dream job has become a daily disappointment. Do we really have to face a job we hate every single day, just because it is a quick commute, or because we worked so hard to land it in the first place?

Or it might be our one-time dream partner who we no longer love and only stay with for the sake of the children. Yet everyone who has children knows very well that they copy our behaviour, whether we want them to or not. What are we teaching our children when we stay in a relationship in which we are no longer happy?

'Dear child, when you have children yourself, sadly you will have to stay with your partner however unhappy you are. Only once all the kids have left home and finished studying do you have a right to your own life!'

Is that what you want to teach your children? No? So why do you teach your children it by example? Do you really want your children to grow up to suffer exactly like you do?

Perhaps none of this applies to you. In that case, it may well be your circumstances, perhaps the urgent need to move home while dealing with a stressful situation with your family, or a circle of friends you simply have nothing in common with any more.

Indeed, with more than 70 per cent of my patients I was able to identify the origin of their anxiety disorder to one of these three issues: relationship, job, or personal circumstances. This means that in seven out of ten cases it is worth taking a long hard look at the balance sheet of the past, in order to find out whether a long-overdue change might not be the solution to the problem. In Chapter 4 I will show you how to gather the strength necessary to change step by step, and what you can do to avoid making the same mistakes in future. There is no need to be alarmed: no one is asking you to take a leap in the dark. The path to health is gentle and consists of many small, easy steps. It all starts with doing something different.

Do you remember the Einstein quote from the beginning of the book? *'The definition of insanity is doing the same thing over and over and expecting different results.'*

Legendary American businessman Henry Ford put it even more succinctly: *'Love it, leave it, or change it.'*

There are three possibilities: love the situation, find a way out, or change it. The first thing you should do, therefore, is to find value in yourself again. For only when you respect yourself, when you love yourself, can you be a source of energy and inspiration for your friends and family. Only when you feel good in your own skin can you be a valuable and productive worker at your company.

Find out what you really need to be happy again. It is not about what other people expect from you; the only thing that matters is what you need. You might call it healthy egoism. But do not forget that you can only get power from a charged battery – being stuck on 0 per cent is not going to help anyone.

Fun and relaxation, not highs and lows

Make a list – today – of the things you would like to do. Going for walks, swimming, painting, reading, having friends round for a barbecue, dancing, listening to music or playing music yourself, whatever it might be. As soon as you think of something you enjoy or you can see yourself enjoying, write it down. Everything on this list has the potential to restore your energy reserves. At this moment you may well be thinking: 'That's easy enough to say, but where am I going to find the time to do all this – I can barely keep up with everything I'm supposed to do as it is?'

This line of thinking is comparable to walking through a long dark tunnel and lighting your way with a torch whose batteries are running out, telling yourself all the while that you do not have time to replace them. Only when you are plunged into complete darkness, groping your way along the cold damp wall completely disoriented, does it become painfully clear that you set the wrong priorities. If you had taken your time to make sure you had enough energy in the tank, you would have got through the tunnel twice as fast. For as a torch with fresh batteries shines much brighter, you will be energised and more relaxed.

Right now, perhaps you are experiencing something common to many of my patients. You realise that off the top of your head, you cannot actually think of very much that would really be fun. However, if I were to ask what you really **do not** want to do, then your mind kicks into gear at once. This is perfectly normal in your situation and nothing you should worry about. Your brain is simply much more used to recognising what you **do not** want than things that do you good. Take a young man who has spent years working out his left arm but does not use his right arm at all, even though both are healthy. While one arm packs on muscle, the other becomes thinner and weaker. After a while, the left arm is capable of lifting 50kg with ease, while the right arm struggles with 5kg.

In your opinion, what does the young man need to do to sort out this imbalance? Correct: he needs to train the right arm and leave the left arm alone for a while. As impossible as it is to make muscles disappear by working out, it's as impossible to solve a problem by letting the same thoughts play on your mind. Much better to apply yourself where you lack muscle – or neuronal networks.

If the young man was to say: 'But I can't train my right arm, it's far too weak. Why can't I just use my left arm, it's so much easier?' you would probably, and correctly, reply: 'That's precisely why you should work on your right arm, stick at it, and you'll see how quickly you progress!'

And this is exactly what I would tell you. Stick at it and train your brain to be able to feel happiness, levity and joy again. To start off with, that is going to be harder than simply numbing the pain with pills and alcohol, but the effort is worth it. For most patients, just 20 minutes of daily mental training is enough to develop a completely refreshed attitude to life within six weeks. Strengthened in this way, you will be able to recognise which outside influences significantly contributed to your anxiety disorder and you will succeed again in freeing yourself from them, step by step.

Summary: stopping panic attacks caused by external influences – quickly

- There is a whole series of drugs that can trigger panic attacks. If a substance ever causes you to react with panic, avoid it completely in future.
- Some medications are known to be capable of triggering panic attacks, but in medicine there are almost always alternatives. Discuss them with your doctor, or if necessary find a new doctor who understands the issue.
- If you are currently taking psychiatric medication, please DO NOT stop taking it on your own. Instead, gradually reduce the dose under medical supervision.
- You alone are responsible for your life. Life is too short for a bad relationship, a lousy job, or a living situation in which you do not receive the love and appreciation you deserve. Learn to live your life by this motto: love it, leave it, or change it.

- You can only get power from a charged battery. That makes healthy egoism a prerequisite for being able to do your bit as a life partner, parent and professionally.
- It is not about getting rid of anxiety, it is about surrounding yourself with people and responsibilities that do you good. As soon as you do that, the anxiety will disappear as fast as it came.

4

REWIRING YOUR BRAIN

As anxiety is known to be a learned behaviour, anxiety disorders can almost always be traced back to misrouted automated processes in the brain.

Thankfully, thanks to modern neuroscience we now know much more about how these patterns of behaviour are stored in the brain. Thanks to this new knowledge, methods have been developed to 'unlearn' patterns of behaviour that we no longer want. You may be sceptical, especially if you have already tried other therapies without success, but try to keep an open mind. Using a special mental-training programme, which I describe in detail in this chapter, as well as the Stop Anxiety techniques in Chapter 5, it is possible to completely overcome most anxiety problems within six to 12 weeks.

Anxiety is a learned behaviour

Imagine that a one-year-old is sitting in the middle of a room and playing with building blocks. His mother is sitting watching him, perfectly relaxed. Suddenly a big, strange dog bursts into the room and approaches him. The first thing the child does when he sees the dog is to seek eye contact with his mother. It is not the situation itself, but the mother's reaction that will decide if the baby will be frightened by the dog, or curious about it. If the child sees fear in his mother's eyes, he will be struck with it himself at once, and soon begin to cry. If he sees that his mother is smiling and relaxed, then that means that the dog is not dangerous, and therefore it is safe to touch and engage with.

Responsible for this process are the 'mirror neurons', which all people possess. They see to it that from childhood we copy the behaviour of our attachment figures and through this intuitively learn what is good and bad for us. This is also why children who grow up in a household where dogs are part of the family very rarely develop a fear of dogs.

We humans have only two fears that we are born with: fear of heights, and fear of loud noises. All our other fears are learned over the years, with many of them being formed in the first six years of life.

Learning means forming a sufficient number of synapses on the neuronal level for the behaviour to run automatically. This is why people with a strong fear of change frequently had parents who exhibited similar patterns of behaviour. Parents who, for example, were so averse to change that they may have spent decades building a career that they did not enjoy, or who 'stayed together for the children's sake', even though the relationship had run its course. In these cases, from birth the children could learn certain patterns of behaviour thanks to their mirror neurons reinforcing these neuronal connections time and time again.

And yet something that has been learned can also be unlearned. No one can force you to keep copying behaviour that does not enable the life you want. Thanks to modern neuroscience, there is now a whole range of techniques that can help you with this process. Admittedly, at present these techniques are put to good use far too infrequently. As a result, far too many therapists, not to mention their patients, remain wrongly convinced that it is difficult to free yourself from panic and anxiety.

Why traditional therapies often do more harm than good

Much of what we thought we knew about the brain in the seventies, eighties and nineties has been conclusively disproven by science. Sadly, many current standard therapeutic practices were developed during this time, or even earlier. It should come as no surprise, then, that many people who have spent years being treated using these methods still suffer panic attacks.

Until the mid-nineties, it was 'common knowledge' that the adult brain was practically incapable of change. Thanks to Professor Eric Kandel and many other ingenious researchers, we now know that the exact opposite is the case. Our brain is in a constant state of change, moulding itself every day to the way it is used. For example, one study of taxi drivers in London[7] showed that the area of their brain responsible for spatial memory and navigation is markedly bigger than that of someone who works in an office.

We call this capacity 'neuroplasticity'. However, nearly all traditional forms of therapy were developed at a time when the brain was believed to be incapable of change. Most of these methods are between 30 and 60 years old – and in the case of psychoanalysis, more than 120 years old. Many standard therapeutic approaches are based on the idea that once we reach adulthood, the brain is almost incapable of change.

But we know this isn't true. Just as specific parts of cab drivers' brains markedly increase in size, your brain too reacts to how it is used, day in, day out. Maybe you have spent years worrying. Perhaps criticism is quicker to pass your lips than praise. Were you brought up to be a pessimist? Then your brain will be much more efficient at finding problems than opportunities. It will be a lot quicker to find reasons why a dream can never be realised than to generate ideas that can make it happen. In reality, there are not more problems than opportunities, but your brain has been trained in finding the one and ignoring the other.

A brain that has been trained in anxiety long enough will sooner or later almost inevitably develop an anxiety disorder or depression. And yet, if you can train your brain to be 'good' at panic and anxiety, then it stands to reason that it can be changed to be good at happiness and joy. And indeed, techniques are now available that make 'reprogramming' the brain possible within a matter of weeks. Neuroscientists have a saying: 'Neurons that fire together, wire together.'

With the help of a newly developed form of mental training that you will come to learn in detail in the following chapters, it is now possible to make great numbers of your synapses fire off positive information at once, which leads to them forming connections with each other and building a new, positive information superhighway.

The stronger this new network in your brain becomes, the more frequently you will think positive thoughts automatically, while the anxious ones gradually decrease. Once you have managed to spend three weeks thinking more positively than negatively, your body will actively start helping you to overcome your fears. For from this point on, the laws of cellular renewal start working with you, rather than against you. Another saying familiar to neuroscientists is: 'Use it or lose it!' Just as unused muscle wastes away, muscles grow stronger when trained. In your brain, synaptic connections in which anxiety is stored degrade once they have been neglected for long enough, whereas constantly running these thoughts through your head leads to the anxiety becoming generalised, spreading ever wider on a neuronal level.

You might already be realising why so many standard therapies take unnecessarily long to have a positive impact on anxiety patients. On the one hand, group and exposure therapy, and continuous discussion of the anxieties, simply strengthen neuronal networks that need to be replaced. On the other, the commonly applied relaxation techniques such as qigong, muscle relaxation and autogenic training are 'only' suited to helping you relax a little. They do little to change the real neuronal foundation of your anxiety. And breathing techniques too are, sadly, incapable of quickly reversing negative automated thinking. The fact remains that in the long run, anxiety can only be tackled by going to the source in the neuronal structures of your brain.

Despite all these reservations, I would like to mention a praiseworthy exception. There are many excellent techniques to be found in cognitive behavioural therapy, acceptance and commitment therapy, solution-focused brief therapy, as well as in hypnotherapy, which I use in my clinic on a day-to-day basis. However, I use only those components of these therapies that have been proved to positively stimulate the brain's neuroplasticity. And this is a crucial point that distinguishes my work from that of many of my colleagues. Most of them do a fantastic job, yet they still erect a barrier that hinders much potential healing effect by using methods that above a certain level of anxiety continue to negatively network the brain. One example of this is exposure therapy.

Exposure therapy

Exposure therapy does create numerous neuronal connections in your brain – but unfortunately the great majority are of the wrong kind. How is that possible? During this type of treatment, a therapist guides you through a situation that makes you especially afraid. This is supposed to teach you that your fear is groundless; after all, you survived the situation. The more often you submit yourself to this torture, the more your anxiety should be 'blunted' – at least in theory.

However, this is successful only in the very early stages of an anxiety disorder. In eight out of ten cases, exposure therapy actually makes anxiety even worse. For while on the one hand you learn on an intellectual level that the anxiety-inducing situation does not kill you; on the other you spend hours trapped in a situation of intense anxiety and urge to escape.

Given that each thought creates a neuronal network in the brain, and that these networks become more efficient the stronger the emotions are that underlie the thought, with each exposure session a few hundred positive synapses are created along with many thousands of negative neuronal connections.

It is much smarter to start off by rewiring your brain in a safe environment, after which you will find, completely free of tension, that you can do everything once more without experiencing anxiety. You will find out how exactly this works in Chapter 4.3.

Psychoanalysis

In the case of psychoanalysis, the potential negative consequences for anxiety patients are even more drastic. All of that digging around in childhood memories has one main purpose: to uncover the childhood trauma that is supposed to be responsible for the development as an adult of this or that psychological problem.

It is beyond dispute that developments in early childhood have an influence on the formation of our character and therefore on the remainder of our life. Nevertheless, this influence is less significant than was long supposed. Our genetics are at least as important, as well as our social environment, and even our prenatal development; that is, what we experienced in the womb.

We now know that at least two of these four factors must have been extremely adverse to have had a measurable impact on our later lives. And the impact of these consequences depends heavily on the positive or negative balance of the other factors. This is why, for example, a supportive circle of friends or a sympathetic aunt can do much to counterbalance the damage bad genes or clueless parents might do.

Even if medicine or psychology is completely unfamiliar territory, common sense is enough to tell you that the intense focus of psychoanalysis on various traumatic childhood experiences must be a dead end. For if negative experiences in earliest childhood really were responsible for the development of an array of psychological disorders, then everyone who was a child during the First and Second World Wars would have completely ruined personalities. Strangely though, these very generations were both physically and mentally extremely robust. In fact, it seems that childhood adversity might almost help the human soul mature. When you're next in a bookshop or library, take a look at the biographies of truly outstanding personalities: you will see that almost all of them had a difficult childhood. Of course, please do not take this as a suggestion that you should make your children's lives unnecessarily difficult! Believe me, both the school system and contemporary society do more than enough in that regard.

If we have endured difficult childhood experiences, and our unconscious has decided that they are better forgotten, then we should leave it that way. To quote the doctor and comedian Eckart von Hirschhausen again: 'Maybe your childhood was shit. But what good is it supposed to do if we stick a crock of shit on our lap and spend two years stirring it? It's not going to turn into gold, it's still a crock of shit.'

One of the main tasks of our unconscious is to protect us. To do this, it functions much like a computer's virus scanner. It constantly checks all the information coming in to see whether it is useful, or a potential source of damage. As soon as the program discovers a virus that it cannot delete, it quarantines it. The virus is still present on the computer, but it cannot do any damage any more, because we can no longer come into direct contact with it. The only mistake we could make now is to release the virus from quarantine so we can look at it in perfect detail. And this is exactly what psychoanalysis does.

So there are good reasons why there are circumstances in which we cannot – or do not want to – remember certain things that happened in childhood. Otherwise, our extremely efficient unconscious would have already made those memories available.

In my judgement, psychoanalysis always comes to the same conclusions anyway: 'Your parents are to blame!' But does knowing that really do you any good? Maybe you are mad at your parents now, because they ruined your life. However, if we stick with the logic of psychoanalysis, your parents have the best excuse in the world: there was nothing they could do about it – it was the grandparents' fault! In this manner, responsibility for your own life is continuously shifted to the previous generation, until finally we arrive at the first humans in paradise. Sadly, though, this does not go very far in helping you solve your problems.

Please do not get me wrong. I do not wish to disparage the achievements of earlier generations of therapists. Sigmund Freud did great work when he rethought the human psyche more than 125 years ago, founding psychoanalysis in the process. Based on his work, many new analytical approaches were developed and tested. And it must certainly be an exciting undertaking to work out what your relationship with your parents was and how behaviours learned in early childhood still influence your life. Nevertheless, the techniques of psychoanalysis are starting to show their age, especially since they have not undergone any real development in all that time. Presumably, you would not go to a dentist who still works with instruments that are 125 years old. You should be no more satisfied with an equally antiquated form of therapy in order to rid yourself of an anxiety disorder.

Group therapy

Fundamentally, I do not consider group therapy to be a bad thing. Especially with addictive disorders, it is a good method that can help people to overcome their addictions and support them in avoiding a relapse. For anxiety patients, though, I consider group therapy – at least in the form it is usually offered in – to be completely the wrong option, even dangerous. It is not just that hundreds of patients have already told me that this form of therapy just made things worse for them; from a neurophysiological viewpoint too, group therapy usually does more harm than good to anxiety patients.

Why is this? As we have seen, everything that we think and perceive is stored in our brain in the form of synaptic connections. So what happens when we spend hours sitting in a circle with a group of people listening to them talking about all the awful problems they have with anxiety, and before telling our own anxiety story? During this time thousands upon thousands of neuronal connections develop in your brain, primarily storing one piece of information: anxiety! Over and over again you hear how long everyone else has been struggling with anxiety, how difficult it is to get an anxiety disorder under control and how badly their family and career have already suffered because of it. The only thing you can really learn in group sessions like these is that you are not alone with your anxiety.

In the moment that one understands how the human brain works, group therapy for anxiety disorders stops making sense. It is not as if in groups like these there will also be two or three people telling you: 'Hey, keep your chin up, it was a piece of cake getting rid of my anxiety. I managed to expose and alter my false beliefs with this one simple technique. Everything's going great again, in fact, life's even better than it was before.'

You will not find people like these in group therapy, even if that would be a real innovation. Rather, you will find people who do not know how to free themselves of anxiety talking to other people who do not know how to free themselves of anxiety.

Personally, I would only ask for help from someone who knows their stuff. After all, you would not ask someone without a licence to teach you how to drive a car. No, you'd find a driving instructor. So instead of sitting in a circle and making each other crazy, I'd prefer to surround myself with people who were able to quickly get a grip on their anxiety, and I would ask them how exactly they did it.

Distraction

Distraction is the best known and most frequently used method to get rid of anxiety and panic in the short term. In fact, in the very early phase of an anxiety disorder, this technique is quite useful, but applied to a long-standing illness, it has a decisive disadvantage: it does not prevent, but merely delays the next attack. Whatever you distract yourself with – staring at a pattern or at the leaves of a tree, crunching rows of numbers or memorising street names, or through a telephone conversation with a friend – as soon as you stop, the anxiety is waiting to pounce the next opportunity it gets.

You might compare this method to throwing a boomerang. For a little while it is gone, but after a few yards it turns around of its own accord and if you do not watch out it will crack you on the skull. Say that for a good long while, you have just been distracting yourself when you feel panic, but you are still subject to panic attacks the same as before. That would be like throwing away a boomerang fifty times, and each of those fifty times it came back and hit you on the head. The bump that you have now developed is the direct result of this method. The result is not something you can really be satisfied with. In your case, by the way, this ever-growing bump is called phobophobia: the fear of fear. This too will get bigger and bigger if, instead of tackling the real source of your anxiety, the only thing you do is distract yourself.

You know by now that you are triggering panic attacks yourself because you are permanently waiting for the next one to happen. The thought: 'This would be a really bad time to have a panic attack,' is almost a guarantee that the panic will come. Fear of fear is one of the main triggers of panic attacks, meaning that distraction can never be anything more than a delaying action, never the real solution to the problem.

What would happen, though, if instead of banishing the anxious thoughts, you consciously fixed them in your mind? Well, something that you hold on to is not going to take you by surprise, at least. In fact, you would now have a chance to consciously alter these negative thoughts, feelings and inner images.

I am sure that someone will have said to you: 'You have to face your fear.' Sadly, this very phrase has been misinterpreted not only by anxiety sufferers but also by many therapists for decades. This method is not about letting everything wash over you. On the contrary, it means you should actively work to change the trigger mechanisms for your anxiety. And it is also about understanding that anxiety is nothing but a labour of love by our psyche. A first and important step would be to say to yourself: 'Okay, I've understood that I need to make changes in my life so that my unconscious can finally stop sounding the alarm.' Facing fear always means accepting good advice and making a start on the necessary changes.

The two tiers of successful anxiety therapy

With anxiety disorders, there are two tiers where change can be effected that complement each other.

Tier 1 is changing your circumstances. Your circumstances can include a relationship, job, your social life, even the consumption of certain substances. Once you start making the necessary changes, your unconscious can stop trying to jerk you awake with panic attacks. So that you have the courage necessary to see through change, you would do well to put your brain into 'positive' mode beforehand using the 10 Sentence Method (see page 83).

Tier 2 is direct interaction with the anxiety itself. The longer you have been suffering from anxiety, the more deeply your brain will have automated its sensitivity to anxiety with the physical reactions that occur as a result. You are, as it were, conditioned to react with anxiety in certain situations, even when you already know that the situation is no longer threatening.

You can imagine the chain reaction of anxiety as a row of dominoes. Once the first one starts falling, the rest will follow. Yet if you break the chain by removing one of the dominoes, then it stops there. In psychology, removing a domino is called pattern breaking. To be able to break a pattern in the first place, though, you must first be able to recognise it as such. But how are you supposed to recognise your personal anxiety pattern if you always distract yourself? Only once you have taken a clear look at your anxiety-inducing thoughts, inner images and physical reactions will you be able to recognise the pattern and find the exact spot where the chain reaction of anxiety is easiest to stop.

In my last few years of clinical work I was able to identify more than a dozen common patterns of anxiety. And for each of these patterns there is a pattern breaker. In strongly visually oriented people, for example, anxiety is often triggered by a quickly moving scene in their mind's eye. Some might picture themselves falling over, or trapped in a situation they cannot escape from. Others see themselves having an accident while driving or having a nervous breakdown while flying. The anxiety triggered by inner imagery has a common pattern – the images always come very quickly. And this is the weak spot of visually triggered anxiety.

Have you ever been to the cinema? Perhaps to see a horror movie where the killer is hiding in the bushes with knife drawn, until quick as a flash he pounces on a victim? Wouldn't that give anyone a shock? The whole thing only works, though, when the killer attacks suddenly. If the entire scene were to play out in slow-motion, then no one in the cinema would be scared. The film would soon get boring, and within five minutes most of the audience would have left the cinema.

Visually triggered anxiety, then, has a fatal weak spot – it only works when the images move quickly! Still, how does this realisation help to formulate a fast and effective therapy method to stop the anxiety? I answer this question in detail in Chapter 5, where you will find all the fantastic techniques and pattern breakers with which many patients have already managed to free themselves of anxiety for ever.

A word of caution: do not forget that anxiety itself, as well as all the physical symptoms that come with it, is usually a warning signal from your unconscious that you urgently need to make changes in your life. Simply using these new techniques to rid yourself of all the unpleasant feelings and associated anxiety you have without thinking to enquire why your psyche sounded the alarm would be a mistake. That would be like turning off that annoyingly beeping smoke alarm when your house is on fire instead of putting the fire out. In terms of psychosomatic illness, putting the fire out means rewiring the brain and stopping the neuronal information superhighway of anxiety. The is the basis of your fear of change and hence the real cause of your anxiety disorder. Since you built this superhighway yourself by thinking in a certain way, you will need the blueprints for a new, better information superhighway in your brain, along with Stop Techniques (see Chapter 5) for the symptoms. And that is exactly what is coming up next.

The 10 Sentence Method: how to reprogramme your brain

The fastest way to free yourself for ever from anxiety and panic is a two-pronged strategy: quickly stopping anxiety using the appropriate pattern breakers, and creating new neuronal networks. In this way you can stop the anxiety from returning by robbing it of the fertile soil it needs to grow.

The quickest way to do it is using a special mental training system called the 10 Sentence Method. The idea at the heart of this system is based on a simple question: 'What would your life be like if your life was amazing?' When I ask my patients this question, I often hear just two words: 'Panic-free!' More often, my patients do not know what to say at first. If I ask them what they do not want in their life any more, though, then almost all of them talk for minutes.

Try this test on yourself. Take three minutes to list everything about your life that no longer brings you joy. After that, spend three minutes describing how your life will be once it is amazing. While doing the second part of this test, it is very important to use only positive formulations. After all, we already had a collection of things that you would rather do without in the first three minutes.

While most of my patients find the first task relatively easy, they often struggle to find anything to complete the second. This is further proof that the brains of anxiety patients are better networked for negativity than positivity. Yet there is no need to worry: even if you have been thinking more negatively than positively for many years, that certainly does not mean you need to spend years practising to be able to think differently. Modern neuroscience has developed a technique that allows the brain to be reprogrammed much more quickly than 'standard' thinking would allow. This technique is a major component of the 10 Sentence Method and means you can spend around 20 minutes a day on it and still feel significantly better just three weeks from now. With this boost, you will no longer be in any doubt that your anxiety issues can soon be completely resolved.

As I have already mentioned, the 10 Sentence Method is based on a simple, fundamental question: 'What would your life be like if your life was amazing?' To find out, write down on a piece of paper ten sentences that describe your idea of a perfect life. Before you start, it is important to bear in mind five simple rules, because after all this is about far more than just positive thinking. We want to achieve 'genuine re-programming' in your brain, which means you need to pay close attention to the rules that govern how your brain actually works.

Thinking is an auditory process, for when you think you hear your voice in your head. If that has never occurred to you before, you can test it out here and now. Please think this following sentence five times in a row before reading on: 'I'm really happy that I will be healthy again soon!'

Did you notice? Not just that you heard the sentence in your voice in your head, but that you probably felt your energy level go up just a little bit. What we tell ourselves in our thoughts instantly influences our feel-ings. In this manner the language we use, whether spoken aloud or just thought, really does have the same function as the operating system of a computer. It is the foundation upon which we build everything else. In fact, every single word counts for far more than you can probably imagine at this moment, yet this is one of the main reasons why the methods that you will learn in the rest of this book are so successful.

I will now introduce you to five simple rules that will guide you in how to best use the inner voice of your thoughts to optimally rewire your brain. Once you have mastered and applied these rules, your life will start changing for the better at a speed adherents of old-school anxiety therapies would consider impossible.

RULE 1: 10 SENTENCES, NO NEGATION

'Without negation' means that your sentences must not contain any negatives. NO fear and WITHOUT anxiety would be two typical examples of negation. But why are these negatives a mistake? Because your brain simply is not capable of thinking in negation. Let's try another little test:

Please do **not** think about a bear riding a bicycle. He is **not** wearing sunglasses and he does **not** have a yellow rucksack on his back.

Well, did you manage to avoid seeing the bear in your mind's eye? Of course not. For the thing is, you cannot NOT think. In order to process a piece of information about all the things you are not supposed to think about, first of all you have to imagine it, and in this way network your brain in a particular manner. This means that every time you say to yourself that you do NOT want to have any more panic attacks, you are merely ensuring that your brain is more susceptible to panic, because you have reinforced the panic connections in your brain.

As this book goes on I will challenge you to take more of these small tests. The last thing I want is for you to simply accept what I say unchallenged. Please stay critical and evaluate everything that I have to say for yourself. I'm sure you have already spent long enough taking supposed experts at their word without being freed from your anxiety as a result. So I want to encourage you to take full responsibility for your life again. Learn to understand your own personal anxiety mechanisms – and by doing so learn how to know yourself better. Taking this path will gradually increase your feel for how to programme yourself day in day out with your use of language. Without exception, this self-programming controls all aspects of your life. That is why the techniques in this book do not just help you to transform anxiety into calm, they also put you in a position to achieve significantly more successes than failures in future.

RULE 2: ONLY POSITIVE FORMULATIONS

This rule comes automatically by sticking to Rule 1. Instead of saying: 'I do NOT want to be anxious any more,' from now on say: 'I am brave and self-confident.'

Just as in the first sentence your brain is forced to recall a situation in which you were anxious, in the second it needs to refer to times you have already been brave and self-confident.

Be careful not to use any hidden negatives like 'care-free' or 'debt-free'. It is not just that they contain the negative words 'care' and 'debt', but here the word 'free' is a synonym for 'without' – another way of saying 'no'. Instead of saying 'carefree', you should say: 'I live completely in the here and now and enjoy every single moment.' You could turn 'debt-free' into the following phrase: 'I always have enough money to be able to afford what I need and what is important for me.'

Right now, you might be thinking: 'How is rewording what I think supposed to put more money in my pocket?' Since I get this question a lot, I will give a brief explanation. By thinking differently, you activate different capacities in your brain. Previously, you used much of your time and energy asking yourself why life is so difficult. If you were to use these same resources every day to find new ways to make an easier life possible instead, then you would quickly achieve different results.

At the moment, that might all sound rather esoteric. But the scientific explanation is easy to follow: your unconscious processes more than 80,000 pieces of information per second. You might compare this to 80,000 assistants who are waiting for you every morning to give them their marching orders for the day. As long as they keep getting the order every morning to focus on everything that is standing in the way of your personal success and a brave and self-confident life, that is exactly what your 80,000 unconscious assistants will keep doing. Just imagine how different your life might be if your brain was unconsciously seeking out opportunities to fast-track you to a happier, more rewarding life 80,000 times a second instead.

RULE 3: FORMULATE YOUR TEN SENTENCES IN THE PRESENT TENSE

We now know thanks to modern neuroscience that our brain forms large numbers of synapses when we experience something in real life. What is much more exciting, though, is that we form almost as many neuronal connections when we intensely visualise something. As soon as we start thinking that we are already capable of doing everything that we want to achieve, it really does start getting easier to achieve those goals in reality.

This phenomenon has already been exploited successfully for years in top level sport and is a significant aspect of mental training. Take an ice skater who wants to learn a new, complicated figure. Her coach would ask her to visualise the figure being performed perfectly, over and over again. Sometimes he would put the focus only on how the routine looks, on other occasions he would draw attention to how it feels. How does each individual muscle feel in the moment that the ice skater performs the figure perfectly? The important thing to note here is that she acts in her thoughts as if the desired situation were already reality. Studies have shown that adding mental training in sports can speed up training success by up to 40 per cent compared to purely physical training.

If something already works well in sports, all the more reason to apply it to your own health and well-being. So please formulate your ten sentences exclusively in the present tense, even if you believe it might take years for you to achieve these goals. Nor must your sentences focus exclusively on your physical or mental well-being. Ordinary, everyday goals and achievements are perfectly suited to putting your brain back on the right track in short order. 'I'm enjoying a dream holiday in the Maldives' and 'I live with a wonderful partner' are just two possible examples of a life you might want.

RULE 4: PHRASE YOUR SENTENCES IN CONCRETE TERMS

The more tangibly you describe your dream life, the faster your brain can create the necessary neuronal connections. Vague generalities like 'I feel good' or 'I am happy' offer too little for your grey cells to be able to network quickly and extensively. Find phrases that describe concrete future situations that you wish to experience as soon as you have overcome your anxiety. Concentrate on areas of your life where avoidance behaviours are already par for the course. For example, if you have not been able to drive a car for a long time, a good phrase might be: 'I love going for a spontaneous drive in my car.' Here are some more examples of how your concrete sentences might look:

- I wake up in the morning rested and ready to take on the world.
- I love my new job, have a lot of fun with my lovely colleagues and every day I think about how happy I am that my work is so valued there.
- I drive a great car that gives me pleasure every day.
- I cook for friends and enjoy being a good host.
- I treat myself like my best friend. I speak to myself with respect, eat well and surround myself only with people who do me good.
- I enjoy playing my favourite sport twice a week and feel really good in my body.
- I enjoy being social and it is really easy to greet everyone with a friendly smile. I love the positive energy that I get in return thanks to behaving this way.
- I maintain friendships old and new and every day I am overjoyed at how many lovely and inspiring people there are in my life.

- I enrich my life with many wonderful activities such as [please add concrete examples here] and am pleased with how much my horizons are being extended every week.
- I treat my mind only to good information that helps me to make my life even easier, more joyful and more successful.
- I have turned my hobby [use your real hobby here] into my job and love making good money through something that I really enjoy.

RULE 5: MAKE SURE YOUR SENTENCES ARE 'SELF-ACHIEVABLE'

That does not mean that your sentences should only contain 'realistic' goals. On the contrary, the higher you set the bar, the faster you will achieve success. That might sound contradictory at first, but the neuroscientific explanation is actually quite simple. More on that on page 108.

Self-achievable means that your goals should not be dependent on other people. Your boss is not responsible for your life. Nor is your partner, your family, or the government. You alone decide anew every day what you will do next, and with whom you will spend your time.

Often, I have people sitting across from me in my clinic who complain during their first session about how terrible their working conditions are and what a heartless guy their manager is. Then I ask them who made the decision to spend years working for this heartless tyrant, and who made the decision not to look for a better job elsewhere. Very often the only response is a mumbled: 'Me?'

Do you still remember Angela's story from Chapter 3? She spent years telling herself that it was too hard to find a better place to work. The more often she repeated this negative self-programming, the worse her situation got. Yet within two weeks of changing her inner dialogue, she had a new, superior job prospect lined up.

Let's take a closer look at Rule 5 using this concrete example. For the sake of argument, let's say that you have been unhappy at work for many years because of an unpleasant boss, and your sentence would be: 'I feel completely happy in my current job.' That would be a textbook example of a falsely understood positive affirmation, which cannot possibly work in this form. This sentence would not be SELF-ACHIEVABLE, because someone else would have to change for you to be happy again. Thinking this way will merely give you an unpleasant feeling of dependency and helplessness: you would be making your happiness dependent on the behaviour of your boss – probably not the wisest move as chances are your feelings are totally irrelevant to him. His main concern is that you do the most work possible for the least pay he can get away with.

The following phrases, however, are all things you could achieve yourself: 'I have a good job where I and my abilities are valued, and I am appropriately well compensated.' Now it is down to you to work out what your talents are and what exactly this job would look like where you could finally reach your potential. As soon as you know, your 80,000 unconscious assistants can finally get to work. Your brain now has a worthwhile search request to work on and can fine-tune your unconscious perception so that in future you will not let any opportunities pass you by that will lead you to this perfect job.

Many anxiety patients are very clear on what they do NOT want. They do not want a boss who can only criticise, and they do not want a boring and unsatisfying job that is badly paid. Yet this too is giving their unconscious a search request, but one that merely delivers more of what they do not want. That is why people who think this way can usually only find jobs that are barely any better than the one they have already. The same universal laws apply, by the way, to relationships. So long as you keep telling your unconscious everything you do NOT want, you will continue to meet people with these exact negative characteristics.

The 5 Senses Technique: the turbocharger for psychological well-being

Now that you have written down your ten sentences, the next thing to do is rewire your brain as quickly as possible. To do this we will make use of a little trick derived from modern neuroscience, which I like to think of as the turbocharger for psychological well-being. Every day, spend 20 minutes on one of your ten sentences, and as you do so, concentrate on one of your five senses in turn.

You will see, hear, feel, smell and taste one after the other, keeping each sensation as separate as you possibly can. This way of thinking does demand a little practice, but most of my patients still manage to integrate this quick but effective mental training into their lives within less than a week. For example, let's take the following sentence:

'I live in a joyful relationship and am full of happiness every day because of the wonderful and respectful person I am privileged to spend my life with.'

Important: if you are certain that this is never going to happen with your current partner, then please use a fantasy person in this exercise, someone you don't know – yet. If you were to think of a real person, Rule 5 would come into effect; that is, the sentence is not self-achievable. What matters here is simply the human qualities that your dream partner should possess, not a particular person.

A particularly simple and effective move is to mention a concrete situation within the sentence that you would consider part and parcel of a perfect relationship. That might be a relaxing Sunday breakfast together, for example, a walk in the woods, a night of passion, or a visit to the cinema followed by a meal in your favourite restaurant. In the weeks ahead you will always have the chance to pick new scenarios to add to your mental training, as long as they fit the basic idea of a happy relationship. You must bear in mind, though, that you need to use positive formulations. Maybe you think part of a good relationship is having a good argument from time to time. But even the word 'argument' itself is loaded with negativity and therefore off-limits.

Using a visit to the cinema as an example, I will now show you the best way to keep the senses separate. But before I do, there may be some of you who are thinking: 'Of all the things he might choose. I can't go to the cinema any more because of my anxiety.'

You should be aware that the only reason you can no longer go to the cinema is that your brain is planning for the eventuality of you having a panic attack there. It generates images of you sitting panicking in the packed cinema and not being able to leave the auditorium fast enough. It storyboards scenes of you being tsked at reproachfully for squeezing your way through the narrow rows of seats so you can finally get outside. I bet you can hear the snide remarks of the other cinemagoers as well.

At the moment it is still 1,000 times easier for your brain to call up all these negative sounds and images than it is to generate a single positive thought.

But that will soon be at an end – thanks to the following exercises. This is not about forcing yourself to go to the cinema despite your anxiety, but rather first teaching your brain in a safe environment to finally think positively, instead of negatively.

If you work with these techniques for a few weeks, you will soon easily be able to do all the things again that you now believe are impossible. In fact, it is not the worst thing in the world if right now you do not truly believe you can change for the better so quickly, for you will still find that is exactly what happens to you as soon as you start putting the effort into the following exercise.

Find somewhere quiet, make yourself comfortable and go through your five senses one after the other. Try to do this exercise in your head rather than in writing; after all the point is to train a new way of thinking. Anyone who struggles to concentrate at first can use pen and paper to start off with, but a basic principle of the exercise as you go on is to spend this time thinking instead of writing.

To successfully put the 10 Sentence Method into practice with the help of the 5 Senses Technique, let's use the example of going to the cinema. In your thoughts go to your favourite cinema with your partner – or potential partner – and start concentrating only on the visual sense: SEEING. Take your time. The point is not speed, but to immerse yourself as deeply as possible in each of the five senses.

It doesn't matter if you do not have a partner at the moment; simply picture to yourself the characteristics they would need to have for you to fall in love with them.

Once you have consciously envisaged all of the beautiful images that came to mind, switch to the auditory channel, HEARING, and take your time to consider everything you would hear during a perfect trip to the cinema with someone dear to you. Afterwards, switch to FEELING, then SMELLING, and finally to TASTING.

The last two sensory channels in particular activate ancient parts of the brain, making them especially powerful for reprogramming, which is why you should be careful not to stop too quickly once you reach this stage. Additionally, around 98 per cent of anxiety is produced in the first three sensory channels, meaning that both taste and smell are largely free from ingrained anxiety structures and therefore very effective right from the start at positively reprogramming your brain.

THE 5 SENSES TECHNIQUE IN PRACTICE: 'A NICE EVENING AT THE CINEMA TOGETHER'

Here is a concrete example of how to do this exercise in your head. Feel free to change any details to fit your personal preferences. Anyone who does not like cola should simply choose the drink that they would most enjoy drinking in this situation: water, beer, champagne or coffee are all perfectly fine. What we are trying to do after all is mentally plan and wire in behaviour that describes your life when it is thoroughly enjoyable. In contrast, you already have complete mastery of a life ruled by anxiety, which is precisely what we want to avoid reinforcing. So if, for example, you really enjoy drinking coffee, but are currently avoiding it because of your anxiety issues, then now is the perfect time to – at least mentally – start drinking it again. Also of importance is that you do not just mechanically list the individual details, but live them as intensely as possible in your thoughts.

SEEING: I see the cinema auditorium, the big screen, the trailers are already running, I can see the people with drinks and popcorn, I see my own bag of popcorn and my ice-cold cola, I see my partner, how excited they already are waiting for the film to begin, I see them gently reaching for my hand and stroking it, I see their wonderful smile, I watch the film start, see my favourite actor …

HEARING: I hear the dialogue in the film, the music, the audience laughing, the quiet rustle of my popcorn, I hear the gentle creaking of my seat when I move in it, I hear my companion whispering a witty remark to me, I hear my own inner dialogue about how happy I am to finally have such a wonderful person by my side, I hear the popcorn crunch as I bite down on it …

FEELING: I can feel my comfortable seat, I feel how the temperature is pleasantly warm, my partner's hand is soft in mine, I can feel the coolness of the drink I am holding, I can feel the crunchy popcorn in my mouth, I can feel the anticipation as the film starts, I feel good, because I can do all the things that I want to again, I feel the ice-cold drink going down that is so wonderfully refreshing with every sip …

SMELLING: I take in the smell of the auditorium, my partner's perfume, my fresh popcorn, my cola …

TASTING: I taste the popcorn, the cola, my partner's tender kiss …

Perhaps you have already noticed just from reading these few lines how powerful this other way of thinking is. The more details that occur to you as you run the situations through your head, the faster you will be able to lead a happy and carefree life again, for this technique rewires your brain at a speed that outdoes conventional thinking by a factor of 10,000. For while the sentence: 'I'm spending a lovely evening with my sweetheart at the cinema' only generates a handful of synapses in your brain, keeping the five sensory channels separate activates five separate parts of your brain. As soon as you switch from one sense to another, these regions have to start sharing data with each other, since you now not only want to see something, but also hear, feel, smell or taste it. This forces your neurons to fire together repeatedly, which leads in turn to them forming synaptic connections with each other.

Assuming you can find 20 details for seeing, then another 20 each for hearing and feeling, and perhaps ten things that you can smell, as well as five things that you can taste, then during this process your brain cannot help but create 20x20x20x10x5 synaptic connections.

So, have you already worked it out? If you perform this exercise conscientiously, you can generate up to 400,000 synapses in your brain within 20 minutes, all embodying one piece of information: enjoying going to the cinema again regularly with your perfect match.

Once you have been using the 10 Sentence Method in combination with the 5 Senses Technique for a couple of days, you will have realised that sticking to one sensory channel is not as easy as it might seem. Perhaps when you imagine smelling something the wonderful scent of freshly cut grass spontaneously comes to mind. If your sentence was: 'I love going for walks on my own', then your brain cannot help but activate the visual channel and add the freshly cut lawn and the neighbour with the lawnmower, while in the auditory channel you automatically recall the sound of a lawnmower as well, which also leads to new connections being formed.

Jumping from one channel to the other like this is not the end of the world, because this too will create plenty of new positive connections in your brain. The important thing to remember is to return to the sensory channel you started with afterwards, and keep seeking out more things that you will soon be experiencing again once you have overcome your anxiety for good.

As far as taste is concerned, it makes sense, starting with visual exercises, to bring it into situations where eating and drinking is taking place right from the beginning. Assuming you are planning to finally find a job that is truly fulfilling, you might build your lunch break with your lovely new colleagues into the exercise.

Some people can find one or other of the individual techniques a little difficult to start off with. Do not let that put you off – after all you are learning an entirely new way of using your brain. As with everything that you learn from scratch, practice makes perfect.

Since I have observed in my workshops that anxiety patients who have been living with their symptoms for a long time often benefit from being able to SEE the techniques put into practice, I have developed a video course to accompany this book, more on which you can find on my website www.the-anxiety-cure.com.

First successes, and what you can do to improve even faster

As a rule, the 10 Sentence Method combined with the 5 Senses Technique produces its first successes very quickly. In nine out of ten cases that I have handled up to now in my clinic, the frequency and intensity of panic attacks is reduced by around 60 to 70 per cent within the first week. In the case of people who practise the exercise directly before going to bed, the success rate is even higher. There is a very good reason for this: while you sleep, you go through sleep cycles. Somewhere between four and six times a night you switch between deep sleep and dream sleep – the REM phase. In the REM phase, our brain learns, processing the events that we experienced during the day. The brain prefers to process the things we experienced and therefore remembered directly before going to sleep in the REM phase. Just like that, the 400,000 positive neuronal connections that we consciously created for ourselves that evening become up to 1.2 million because we purposely stimulated synapse formation in REM sleep.

Of course, such a rapid structural transformation of your grey cells is not without consequences. Eight out of ten of my patients report their dreams being strongly affected, overwhelmingly, from the third night on. Two out of ten report feeling gentle pressure in their head for a few days, which is completely harmless and soon passes. The particularly sensitive can clearly feel their brain rewiring at high speed. After just a week, general feelings of happiness increase, and you will soon start feeling comfortable in your skin for no apparent reason.

Naturally, there will still be phases in which you will feel anxiety or dissatisfaction. As time goes by, though, these will become shorter and less intrusive.

After around three weeks of consistently working on this exercise, your brain recognises a repeating pattern and starts to deposit certain pieces of information in the cerebellum rather than the cerebrum. The cerebellum is where automated processes are stored. From now on, you are automating calm and happiness where once panic and anxiety held sway.

After six months of mental training, around 70 per cent of my patients are more or less free of anxiety. Those who prefer to conduct their mental training before going to bed make up the majority of this group. A further 25 per cent need another three to six weeks to start living a life without panic attacks and constant fear of fear. From my clinical experience so far, this is how things stay, with a relapse rate of just 5 per cent. Those few who fell prey to panic and anxiety again were victims either of secondary gain (Chapter 1.4.), or simply did not stick with the exercises long enough.

Whether you want a fit, attractive body, or a brain that finds it easy to feel happy and joyful, there is something you can do. If a young man spends two years exercising several times a week, he will surely cut an impressive figure. The stupidest thing he could do now is to rest on his laurels and give up exercising. Within just a few short months, all that hard-won muscle mass will disappear, for our body only retains the muscle that is used regularly. Everyone familiar with working out will be aware of the need for maintenance training two or three times a week to prevent muscle mass diminishing.

Similar laws apply to a brain that has successfully been trained to be receptive to happiness, success and positivity. Only, in this instance, training does not target muscle fibres but synaptic connections. Here too, it is crucial to continue in the same vein even once you feel right as rain again. Therefore, you should keep doing the 10 Sentence exercise for five minutes each evening, or 15 minutes at least three times each week, even if you have been feeling better for months. This is particularly important if you have been tapering off one or more prescriptions during this time, medication that you may long have been habituated to. Your brain needs all the support it can get to successfully wean itself off these psychoactive substances.

By the way, there is another parallel to building muscle. Someone who works out a lot will increase the weight at regular intervals so that the growth process does not stagnate. Therefore, once one of your first ten sentences has become reality, you too should add weight by replacing it with a new one – something else that you would love to experience. You can write down the sentence that you have already accomplished in a success diary, and you will find that this diary fills up a lot faster than you might think.

Here is another important tip to use this method correctly: before you go to bed every evening, use a different one of the ten sentences. After ten days you should have gone through everything on your list, then you can start again from the beginning. If you fall asleep a lot while doing the exercise, start doing it before you clean your teeth. Alternatively, you could also spend two days on each sentence before changing. In this case, you'll need 20 days to get through your list of ten sentences. On the second day of each sentence, you must always work in reverse: start with taste, then smell, then feel, followed by hearing and finally seeing. In this manner, you ensure that you are optimally wiring your brain and that exercise will produce results quickly and effectively.

Many of my patients have also reported that practising the 10 Sentence Method in the evening has an additional positive effect. Those who have had difficulty sleeping find that they can suddenly fall asleep much more easily, and that the quality of sleep also improves week on week.

With the 10 Sentence Method, more is more! There is nothing stopping you repeating the exercise during the day. As was mentioned in the preceding chapter, it is also possible to work through each of the five senses in writing from time to time. I can especially recommend getting individual points down in writing to start off with for people who struggle to concentrate on the exercise. Please make absolutely sure, however, that you do not *just* work through the exercise by writing. After all, this is about integrating a new way of thinking into your daily life, and you do not write down everything you think, do you? Besides, the longer you practise the exercise, the better you will be able to concentrate on it, because you will be training your powers of concentration at the same time.

Summary: finally free of fear with the 10 Sentence Method

- Write down ten sentences about your amazing future life.
- Play by the rules: no negatives, only positives, formulate each sentence in the present tense, make the situations concrete and self-achievable.
- Work through one of the ten sentences in your mind every evening, using the 5 Senses Technique.
- To start off with you may do the exercise in writing, but you should be doing the exercises more and more in your head as you go along to achieve the best possible training effect.
- After ten days, start again with the first sentence, until one of the sentences becomes reality. Then replace this sentence with a new one, that is, a new wish you would like to make reality.
- Ensure that each sentence describes a situation where there is something to smell and something to taste. This accelerates neuronal growth and therefore the healing process.

- DO NOT just read out the sentences. Instead, LIVE the individual situations in your thoughts as intensely as possible.
- Do not stop doing the exercise once you start feeling better, but continue with 'maintenance training' to prevent potential relapses.
- DO NOT choose sentences that already feel easy, because these lack neuronal growth potential. Rather, choose situations that you have not previously achieved or actively avoid, and phrase them as if you were already enjoying them to the maximum.

5

DEALING WITH
EMERGENCIES: FIRST AID
IN SECONDS

Do you still remember the story of the penguin in the desert? In Chapter 2.6. it served to vividly illustrate that the quality of your questions alone decides whether you receive productive answers or not. That is, people who keep asking how the poor creature ended up in the desert are leaving it standing exposed to the sun and suffering for longer than necessary. In contrast, those wanting to know how to get the penguin back to the water as fast as possible will soon be able to work out a solution and actually help.

What this means for you in concrete terms is this: stop wallowing in the past. Instead of trying to dig up some event that supposedly triggered your anxiety, you are better off concentrating on all the fantastic new techniques that are already available to quickly rid you of anxiety and panic.

The one thing that can still stand in the way of your rapid recovery is dogma that someone fed you, perhaps years ago. Things like: 'You can't just get over anxiety in a few weeks' or 'You'll never solve your problems without knowing what caused them in childhood.'

So long as you continue to give these antiquated beliefs any credence, it will remain unnecessarily difficult for you to accept new and innovative methods with an open mind. Yet all it takes is a quick glance back at human history to see that at first, most great discoveries were either laughed at or even violently attacked. Much of what was for decades considered standard medical and therapeutic practice is forgotten today, because there are simply superior methods that have replaced it. Anyone who closes themselves off from new methods as a matter of principle has learned nothing from human history. Anyone who says: 'This and only this way works!' will automatically be put right within the coming year or decade.

It has always been this way and it will always stay this way because people will never stop researching. The only thing that increases is the speed with which the supposedly 'correct' knowledge is replaced by new insights. The famous chemist and two-time Nobel laureate Linus Pauling boiled this connection down to the following well-known quote: *'Science is error brought up to the latest standard.'*

It can be necessary to throw the ballast of old convictions overboard in order to achieve quick successes. It is possible that other therapies have taught you that you have to accept your fear, or you may have even been challenged to give your panic a name, for example, Hugo or Suzie. If any of these methods had been a success, then you would hardly be reading this book, so just go ahead and forget all of that. Unfounded fear is and remains unpleasant, and that is why it is important to overcome it as soon as possible. So it is best to do exactly what you would do in sport when you want to overcome an opponent: you study their weaknesses and exploit them.

In your case, your opponent is anxiety. And even it has a series of weak points that depend on the sensory channel the anxiety is primarily unleashed by. Using the following emergency techniques that I have tested and refined over the years in my clinic, it is possible to stop nascent panic within seconds. However, it's first necessary to find out the greatest weak points of your very personal fear structure with the help of several simple tests.

Following this, you learn several 'pattern breakers' with which you can interrupt the chain reaction of anxiety saved in your brain. This technique works immediately and the positive effect lasts longer the longer you practise it. The anxiety-inhibiting effect of the pattern breaker is so unbelievably strong that by the second session many of my patients already report that the technique has helped them more than all their previous medication and years of therapy did. Of course, such success is only possible if you really open yourself up to it. Anyone who says from the start: 'There's no way that such simple techniques with such powerful effects haven't been put to use long ago in other therapies' unfortunately blocks the necessary psychosomatic effects with this very statement.

However, anyone who is prepared to open up to something new soon has effective tools with which they will always be able to free themselves from anxiety and panic. In this way, 'phobophobia' – the fear of fear – also disappears within a few weeks. For whoever has learned to stop anxiety within seconds is no longer afraid of being unexpectedly seized by it. And that is precisely what ensures that anxiety becomes ever more a stranger before finally vanishing from your life completely.

An important note, in case you are already taking medication for anxiety: do not let the initial euphoria lead you to stop taking all medication prematurely. It is possible that your brain is already so accustomed to these substances that a sudden discontinuation can lead to very unpleasant side-effects. You should have been feeling in top form again for at least six weeks before you can begin to carefully reduce the medication in consultation with your doctor.

Sensing anxiety

We activate all of our fears with the help of our five senses, although 99 per cent play out in one of the following three channels: seeing (visual channel), hearing (auditory channel) and feeling (a combination of kinaesthetic, touch and proprioceptive perception, depending on whether you feel a movement or something on your skin or within your body). However, for simplicity's sake I will speak simply of the kinaesthetic channel from now on.

The visual channel unleashes fears in the form of images that flash in front of your mind's eye. For example, you see yourself faint, have an accident, or make a fool of yourself. These images usually pass very quickly. Sometimes so quickly that you are not even aware of them. That is why it is important in future to pay close attention to precisely how your anxiety is triggered. Every time you are gripped by anxiety, you should ask yourself: 'How did I just trigger my anxiety? Was it a fleeting image, was it a feeling I was especially sensitive to, or was an inner dialogue the trigger?'

With inner dialogues you trigger anxiety or even panic via the auditory channel; in other words, what you tell yourself in your thoughts. Only very few people are aware of it, but as I mentioned on page 85, thinking is an auditory process because when we think we hear a voice in our head. For example, you can say to yourself in your thoughts: 'Hopefully I won't get a panic attack now' or 'I can't handle it, I just can't take it!' Anyone who has any experience with panic attacks can confirm that such thoughts generally only worsen the fear instead of reducing it.

Now maybe you are saying to yourself: 'But I can't even control these thoughts, they just come over me!' You will also have perceived these thoughts with the voice in your head. And this thought too will be very powerful, because it will make you despair and rob you of energy. But luckily this idea is wrong. You can control your inner dialogue. You just have not been shown how to yet. But that will soon change over the course of this chapter.

Kinaesthetically triggered fears arise through certain bodily perceptions that we pay more attention to than we would normally. Once you have been diagnosed with an anxiety disorder, each fleeting muscle cramp and the smallest stomach ache is immediately considered a warning sign, an indication that another panic attack is on its way. But through this very over-attentiveness you activate the release of adrenaline and histamine and ensure that these physical symptoms are amplified. If you did not pay such close attention, then all of these symptoms would disappear just as quickly as they had come, the same way they do for every 'healthy' person, day in, day out.

Kinaesthetically triggered anxiety impacts the bodily functions that are normally automatically controlled by your unconscious, and insidiously at that. For instance, several of my patients try to control their breathing. This inevitably leads to problems because an attempt is being made to control a process that happens automatically for everyone from their very first breath. If we really needed to think to breathe properly, humanity would have gone extinct long ago. Logically, to do breathing exercises is the worst advice you can give patients. Instead of learning to let their body breathe by itself the way it needs to, all their attention is focused on something that should work without conscious assistance.

Incidentally, many of my patients initially claim that their anxiety is triggered on a purely kinaesthetic level. They are not even aware that their unpleasant bodily symptoms are usually preceded by a very short auditory or visual trigger. You might not know this, but anxiety patients PLAN anxiety. Most of them notice this primarily in that they feel okay as long as they are intensely occupied with something. But as soon as they start thinking about if and when they will have another panic attack, the first warning signs appear again. In other words, just thinking about it triggers the next panic attack.

However, anxiety is fundamentally preceded by an inner image and/or an inner dialogue. For example, a brief thought like: 'Hopefully there won't be another panic attack any second' or even a fleeting image in front of your mind's eye, for instance of you lying helplessly on the floor, or quickly running away from a place where you have already had an attack before.

So immediately before anxiety strikes, sufferers actually plan the situation either visually or aurally. However, because many people do not pay attention to what flashes through their heads right before they are overcome by anxiety, the first thing they perceive is the physical reaction. This is expressed very differently according to the individual and can, for instance, appear in the form of dizziness, tingling in the arms and legs, a knot in the stomach, chest pains or a racing pulse.

This insight is very important because many of my patients are convinced that the anxiety came out of nowhere and is expressed purely physically. However, the sooner they realise that it was in fact the preceding negative inner dialogues and images that unleashed the chain reaction of fear, the quicker this chain reaction can be stopped. Nevertheless, in this chapter you will find Stop Techniques that with a little practice you can use to quickly switch off the unpleasant bodily symptoms. Stop Techniques are easy to use methods to stop anxiety symptoms within seconds when they occur. The more effective tools that you have available in your struggle against anxiety, the more quickly the fear of fear will disappear.

However, it would be a mistake to limit yourself to the Stop Techniques. It's only when you disable the real trigger, that is, those thoughts that have been incorrectly wired over the years, that you can truly free yourself from your anxiety in the long term. And that is precisely where the 10 Sentence Method can help you. If you can plan for anxiety so intensely that it triggers a panic attack, you can also learn to plan for calm in order to find your way back to a happy life.

Due diligence obliges me to mention the fears that are triggered by smell or taste. Less than 1 per cent of all anxiety and panic attacks are activated via the olfactory channel (smell) or the gustatory channel (taste). In these cases, the original trigger was usually a traumatic experience in the form of a bad accident, a violent crime or some other misfortune. A smell or a particular taste that was present during such an event can become a trigger for renewed panic attacks and anxiety.

In this case, it may be necessary to not only apply the techniques mentioned in this book, but also rewrite or remove the olfactory and gustatory memories with the assistance of medical hypnosis. If you are one of this relatively small group of anxiety patients, you are certainly welcome to contact our clinic. We are in contact with a series of excellent hypnotherapists we can refer you to.

Pattern breaker: the secret weapon against panic and anxiety

Fear follows certain patterns without our being aware of it. You do not have to study yourself very long before you notice these patterns. Rather, a few simple tests are sufficient, as you will soon discover. But because everyone's fears are constructed in a different way, not all of the typical anxiety patterns will appear with you personally. Some of them will be very clear, some not. First, you should concentrate on the obvious patterns and then train the corresponding pattern breakers so that you can achieve success as soon as possible.

Incidentally, perfectly everyday language can frequently help us find these patterns. Many of the patterns have already been 'hidden' in common language for centuries. A nice example of this would be the so-called 'mental merry-go-round'. There is a reason why we speak about thoughts 'running around our head', because almost everyone who has anything going through their head can observe how they go round and round, clockwise or anticlockwise, like a wheel or a spinning top. Or often like a barrel rolling back and forth, or a spiral winding up and down.

As soon as you have identified your individual direction, you will see that it is a reoccurring pattern. It always turns the same way.

The next time something starts spinning in your head is the perfect time to test your first pattern breakers. First, pay attention to how your mental merry-go-round is turning, and then simply pretend that it is revolving in the other direction. Pay close attention to what happens next. If you can focus well, you will notice the carousel grinding to a halt within just a few seconds. Nevertheless, to start off with make sure you keep concentrating at least ten seconds longer on the reverse direction in your head. Do you notice how quickly you become noticeably more calm and relaxed? For many people, this is the moment when all is calm in their head for the first time in weeks or even months, a nearly magical moment.

Three years ago a friend of mine wanted to visit her brother in a psychiatric ward and asked me to accompany her. The young man had been there for five weeks because he had gone 'haywire'. The mental carousel in his head simply did not come to rest, and he was so worried about losing it completely that he had himself committed.

I've known him since he was little, and that is why he was willing to open up to my unusual question when I asked him to tell me which direction his thoughts were circling. He used gestures to indicate that his mental merry-go-round was heading clockwise. I then asked him to imagine that same carousel rotating anti-clockwise and to focus all his concentration on it. He did this by sitting on a chair and totally withdrawing inside himself while I carefully watched him. After a minute he started to smile, and tears rolled down his cheeks. He stood up, hugged me tightly and said, 'It's quiet. It's all quiet up there, for the first time in weeks.'

From then on, he used this technique whenever his thoughts started to spin. The more he did this, the more quickly calm returned in his head, and the longer the effect lasted. He was ready to be released from medical supervision a week later, and soon returned to his normal life and work.

Testing for your personal anxiety triggers

You will need a couple of pieces of paper and a pen for this test. As an example, we will find two typical anxiety triggers and two triggers for positive feelings. We'll do this by separately examining the three main anxiety channels: sound, then sight, and finally touch. One of these channels is always particularly strongly represented when panic appears in anxiety patients. However, it is still sensible to take a close look at all three channels. Fears tend to jump from one channel to another as soon as an anxiety pattern is broken. Only once you are in a position to target and stop anxiety on all three channels will you be able to quickly and sustainably overcome your anxiety disorder.

Let's start with the auditory anxiety triggers. Write down the two sentences that run through your head most frequently immediately before a panic attack. For instance, they might be: 'Don't panic, not now, it'll be a disaster' or even: 'Oh God, we're heading into a tunnel, hopefully there's not a traffic jam.' Another popular variant is: 'I can't get out of here, I think I'll go crazy.' These are all just examples, so you need to find your own personal inner dialogue and then write down what goes through your head just before or during a panic attack, word for word if possible.

Then you should write down two more sentences you clearly remember where someone told you something that made you very happy. It is important that you still have a good feeling even today when you intensely recall these words. Perhaps you are thinking of your child's voice telling you that you are the best mother or father in the world. Or you remember your boss praising you for something you worked really hard to achieve. Some people enjoy remembering the cries of jubilation from their team after scoring the winning goal. Get started right now and only continue reading once you have the four sentences on the paper in front of you.

Done? Then write AUDITORY at the top of the page and lay it aside.

Take a new piece of paper and write down two situations in which you had a particularly strong feeling of anxiety or panic, and have the images clear in your mind. Where and when was it exactly? Was there somebody with you or were you alone? What happened, what did you see, regardless of whether it was real or just imaginary?

For example, many people immediately see themselves fainting, or driving their car into the other lane, or slamming into the crash barrier. All of this virtually never happens in reality, but just picturing the image is enough to trigger real anxiety. Now write down another situation that is also negative, but where you did not have a panic attack. This incident can be from years ago, for instance an intense fight with your partner, an accident, a particularly painful defeat or something similar.

Now you also need some positive counteracting images so that you can correctly carry out the test. So search through your memory for two positive sequences that you can very clearly picture visually. Many people think of the birth of their first child, an exam passed with flying colours, a fantastic holiday or a dream fulfilled. Please only select clearly positive memories, so no difficult births, no images where you were madly in love with someone if you are no longer with this person or where the love has disappeared and no holiday where you were already tormented by panic attacks.

Perhaps this part of the test might be hard for you at first because you are no longer used to recalling purely positive memories. But if you have been correctly executing the 10 Sentence exercise for some time, then you will not have any difficulties at all, because your brain is already so well rewired. Start right away and continue reading only when you have written down the respective scenes.

Done? Then write VISUAL at the top of this page and lay it aside.

Now all you are missing is the kinaesthetic trigger. Here you use yet another piece of paper to write down all the unpleasant feelings that you can clearly perceive as soon as you feel the anxiety welling up inside. Leave at least two lines between every feeling, because you will need them later.

Please do not use 'racing heartbeat' even if it is your most typical symptom. A racing heartbeat is 'only' the result of adrenaline being released, and disappears by itself as soon as you start actively working with your pattern breakers. In addition, a fast heartbeat is not generally detrimental to your health, even if it feels like it in the moment. Your heart races when you do a vigorous workout, have passionate sex or watch an exciting film. Sport is well-known for its positive health effects. After all, the heart is nothing more than a muscle. And it gets stronger the more it is put to the test. So it ultimately does not matter if your racing heartbeat comes from adrenaline being released, or from a 100-metre sprint. In both cases you are working your heart and simply making it stronger.

Write down all of the other physical symptoms you are able to perceive during an anxiety attack. Perhaps dizziness, a tingling in your arms and legs, tightness in your chest or a lump in your throat. Describe the feelings as precisely as possible, and pay attention to the direction and temperature of the feeling. For example, if you feel ants crawling on your arms, pay attention to whether they are walking up or down your arms, and whether this feeling is hot or cold. If you spontaneously think of a colour, for instance, red, then write that down too. The more details you can associate with the feeling, the easier and quicker it will be for you to stop the feeling later on. Pressure around the belly, for example, can be directed inward or outward. It can be a sharp feeling, like being stabbed with a knife, or a dull feeling like a punch. Vertigo can appear as a dizziness that is circular or goes back and forth. Here as well, a direction can be determined, whether turning clockwise or anticlockwise, or swaying to the left or to the right.

It is quite possible that you may only be able to truly describe your feelings the next time they arise, when you can consciously observe them. If that is the case, then only write down your feelings when the time comes. Try to have the piece of paper with the heading KINAESTHETIC within reach, and regard the next panic attack as what it is: a good opportunity to expose your anxiety's weakness and be able to combat it on this level as well.

Exposing your anxiety's weaknesses

Taking care that you will not be disturbed for several minutes, sit down and pick up the AUDITORY page. The following test is initially very irritating for many of my patients, and some of them need a moment until they have concentrated enough that they can truly listen within. All of them ultimately manage if they only take enough time to find their anxiety's crucial weak spot. So be patient with yourself.

Firstly, read the first two of your anxiety sentences in your head. This may seem a little strange, but pay attention to see if you can perceive which side you can more clearly hear the sentences on. With your left or right ear? If you cannot immediately decide on a side, repeat the sentences until you can clearly recognise a tendency to hear the anxiety sentences on one side. Some people can more clearly locate the negative sentence on one side if they close their eyes during the test. If you happen to perceive the sentences precisely in the middle of your head, then test which side it is easier to shift this inner dialogue to and which side it does not want to go. Then note if you have more clearly received the negative sentences on the left or right side of your head.

Now repeat this test with both positive sentences. Remarkably, around 91 per cent of my patients can very quickly establish two things. First, that the thoughts were, in fact, more clearly heard on one side than the other, and second, that the side changed, depending on whether the focus was on positive or negative thoughts.

Don't worry if you happen to be one of the few people who are not able to determine a respective side. This only means that you prefer other channels for your anxiety, and here, too, there are suitable tests and techniques, which we will come to very soon. Nevertheless, carry out this test to the end, and perhaps you will be surprised after all.

In fact, very attentive people can relatively quickly determine that they are able – at least subjectively – to distinguish between good and bad thoughts according to brain sides. Observations in my clinic have revealed that around 51 per cent of my patients hear the bad thoughts more on the left side, and the good thoughts more on the right. It was exactly the opposite 42 per cent of the time.

Here is where an additional clear pattern emerges: different emotional states apparently prefer to be perceived on differing sides of the brain.

Now pick up the VISUAL page and repeat the test, first with the negative, then with the positive images. Those of you who were able to clearly distinguish a separation on the auditory level will most likely also be able to easily differentiate with images as well. You hear and see negative on one side and correspondingly positive or at least neutral on the other side.

If you still had difficulty with listening, then it is quite possible that you will now be able to recognise a 'good' and a 'bad' side for sight because you are presumably more oriented on the visual than on the auditory channel. The hearing test is also often easier the second time round.

About 7 per cent of my patients cannot perceive a preferred side for either the inner images or the inner dialogues. For them, everything feels like it is in the middle. This phenomenon can primarily be observed with people whose anxiety has already expanded into depression. These patients typically suffer sleep disturbances as well as the so-called morning blues. This means that their mood is generally much worse in the morning than the evening. But please do not let this discourage you. There is also a technique for you, which I will introduce later on.

Incidentally, with an overwhelming majority of my patients who are able to clearly differentiate between a good and a bad side, the negative images as well as the negative inner dialogues are on the same side. Only two out of 100 people split the auditory and visual here as well. In this case, they usually perceive the negative images on the left side, but the negative dialogues on their right side, or vice-versa. However, that has no influence on the effectiveness of the following technique. That is why you should start by taking the time to test out where you perceive what, and then adjust the following exercises accordingly.

In addition to the direction our thoughts turn, you now also know an additional pattern our minds follow in order to create positive or negative thoughts: we separate our heads into good and bad sides. In the next chapter you will find out how you can use these patterns in a targeted manner in order to quickly free yourself of anxiety and panic. With the help of additional pattern breakers, you will bit by bit be able to regain control over your mind, till you are finally able to live your life without anxiety and panic.

Important note: about four out of 100 patients react negatively to the following exercises in the first two or three days. While a quick and clear improvement takes hold in 96 of 100, about four out of 100 react with disquiet. However, this almost always calms down within a few days, and the exercises are all the more effective after that.

Stop techniques for visually triggered anxiety

I will be repeatedly referring to images or scenes that you are to call up in your mind's eye. These can be memories of something you have already experienced or even fantasies. It is possible to have a mixture of both. Generally, you see a sort of film playing in your head, although the anxiety-inducing scenes usually go faster than the neutral or positive ones. Some people need a little practice and concentration to perceive what their brain has done completely automatically up till then. Have a little patience with yourself if it does not work right away. Experience in my clinic has shown that sooner or later nearly everyone is able to consciously perceive these processes in their head, in order to actively change them in the next step.

The Visual Slide Technique

Pick out a negative scene that you can visualise particularly well, regardless of whether you have experienced the scene or if it has only taken place in your imagination. It may be helpful to close your eyes during this exercise. Now pay attention to which side of your head this image is appearing, and then try to slide this image to the other (positive) side of your head. Do the exercise right now, and observe what happens. Do not worry, you cannot do anything wrong. At first the goal is just understanding what your brain does when, where and how.

Please continue reading only once you have done the exercise, so that the following lines do not influence what you perceive. So, now you should recall a clearly negative scene. As soon as it is fully formed, try to slide it to the good side.

Did you do the exercise? What did you notice? For most people, the image gets stuck in the middle, as if it were refusing to go to the other half of your brain. That is completely normal because your brain has never learned to visualise negative images on its other side.

People who are particularly visually gifted are already able to slide the images in this early phase. If you happen to be one of these people, you will quickly notice that the image has to change by itself in order to be slid in the first place. The negative scene has transformed, as it were, so that you can perceive it on the good side. It has to become emotionally neutral at least, or even positive. For instance, if on the left side you perceived a scene in which you are sitting in a car, totally anxious, then you will notice a scene on the right side in which you are sitting in a car completely normally. In other words, as if you did not have an anxiety disorder.

The trick consists in not holding tight the negative images, but allowing them to change. Interestingly, it is not at all necessary to know how they change. You can simply watch your brain at work, and you probably will not believe how easily it calls up only negative scenes on the one side, while on the other side it produces only neutral or positive scenes.

Many of the patients who have been trying to get rid of their anxiety for decades in vain are not immediately able to directly apply this slide technique. But with the help of an additional preparatory exercise even this hurdle can be overcome. In this case, in your mind's eye picture a television on a cart. The television is turned off. Now practise sliding this image from left to right and back.

Slide this imaginary television on the cart all the way to the left and all the way to the right in front of your mind's eye until you have the feeling that the exercise is working well. Only then should you leave the television on the negative side and turn it on with the assistance of your imagination. Call up a memory on the screen that is clearly negative, preferably a scene from your VISUAL paper, and then slide the television back over to the positive side. As soon as it has crossed the middle of your field of vision, interference briefly appears on the screen, and then the image changes. Now pay close attention to what happens. Does the screen remain dark, or does the scene appear in a neutral or even positive version? Even if the television only remains dark at first, it is a huge success, because that means you have already learned how to keep your brain from calling up negative images.

This means you have already learned a first effective Stop Technique.

The more frequently you practise sliding, the more automated your brain's new handling procedure for anxiety-tainted images. And even if at first on the positive side the bad image 'only' disappears, over time you will notice that your brain will start to call up more and more pleasant scenes on the positive side all by itself.

For example, many will then see an image on their left side of how they are helplessly suffering a panic attack and dashing out of the supermarket without having finished shopping. But as soon as you slide that picture to the right, it changes and you see yourself satisfied, leaving the shop with bags of food. Or on your bad side you see how you are searching for a toilet, panicked because your stomach has gone haywire. However, on the good side you look like you are in a good mood, strolling through a pedestrian zone and doing a little window shopping.

Why does this simple technique work and what is the neurophysiology behind it? The sliding from the bad to the good side is a pattern breaker that directly affects the release of adrenaline and histamine. Your brain has spent years 'training' these two neurotransmitters to release precisely when you have pulled a corresponding trigger. That can be an image of anxiety, a negative inner dialogue or even concentrating on an unpleasant bodily sensation. The pattern behind it consists in the fact that it prefers to take place on one side of your head. That is why even the mere sliding of your concentration to the other side of your head is enough to interrupt this pattern that has been trained for years on end. This automatically stops your brain from releasing histamine and adrenaline, and therefore all those negative bodily symptoms that are unleashed by these neurotransmitters.

Alternative to the Visual Slide Technique: the Zoom Technique

There is an additional technique for anyone who is able to clearly see the images but simply cannot deal with sliding from one side to another. Of course, this second technique is also suitable for those who are already proficient at sliding. I call this the Zoom Technique. People whose anxiety disorder has already led to depression can often deal better with this than the slide technique.

It is easiest to explain the Zoom Technique with an example from my clinical work.

A young man came to me for treatment because he was no longer able to drive his car on the motorway. We discovered that his anxiety was primarily triggered by visuals. He immediately had an image pop into his head as soon as he needed to decide whether to take the faster way home – via the motorway – or the supposedly safer, much longer route on ordinary roads. He watched himself getting a panic attack on the motorway and then sitting on the side of the road with his hazard lights on until the anxiety receded. In other words, he literally planned with the assistance of an 'anxiety image' that he would have to go through an unpleasant situation again if he decided to take the motorway. So he chose the circuitous back road route with increasing frequency, until he finally completely avoided the motorway. And that without ever having experienced a panic attack.

About two years later his alternative route was blocked off for several months by roadworks and the next best detour around the motorway would have cost him an entire hour instead of just 20 minutes. Because the young man had already worked out that the 20-minute detour already cost him 83 hours of his valuable free time each year and he was not willing to lose three times as much just because he could not get his anxiety under control, he requested an appointment in our clinic. Together with him, I first developed a positive counter-image in which success and ease dominated instead of fear. In this 'target image' he pictured himself turning off the motorway with pride and arriving home less than five minutes later.

I then asked him to picture his anxiety image very precisely, and as soon as he was able to perceive it in his mind's eye, he had to concentrate on how the image quickly grew smaller and smaller. As soon as he had 'zoomed out' away from his anxiety image so far that it could only be perceived as a tiny dot, the target image was to very quickly emerge from that point. Like a pop-up window in a computer, it was supposed to appear and remain in front of his mind's eye, large, colourful and friendly – almost like a snapshot of his perfect future.

Then he was supposed to think about his anxiety image again, and immediately have it shrink down until it was just a tiny dot from which the positive target image once again emerged in big close up. I had him spend a couple of seconds appreciating the positive energy of the target image and once again asked him to repeat the process.

All told, I had the young man zoom out from the anxiety image and then have the target image appear bold and colourful in his mind's eye seven times. At the end of the exercise, he was to stick with the target image as long as he wanted.

When I subsequently asked him what he thought about the exercise and if he had noticed anything, he remarked with astonishment: 'The fourth time I was supposed to return to the anxiety image I wasn't even able to see it properly – all I saw was something shrinking to a tiny dot, and the fantastic target image automatically zoomed in from it.'

We agreed that he should always use this technique from then on when the anxiety image was on its way. In addition, after using the principles of the 10 Sentence Method and the 5 Senses Technique he told me: 'I love to drive my car on the motorway.'

Less than three weeks later, he followed an inner urge and drove home using the motorway and was surprised at how it was even possible. From that day on, he drove that route, until the weak uneasy feeling that occasionally arose had disappeared completely and he was able to drive without any feeling of anxiety.

The Slow Motion Technique

There is also another technique, where the 'good' and the 'bad' sides do not play any role. Here as well, I would invite you to try out the technique, even if the previous techniques already work quite well for you. The more tools you have available in your fight against fear, the more secure you will feel and the more likely that you will also feel strong enough to end your avoidance habits, step by step.

This technique is called the Slow Motion Technique and is based on the fact that the images of fear pass very quickly in our brains. In Chapter 4.3, I already illustrated this with the example of a visit to the cinema. If you are watching a thriller, then you primarily get scared when something happens quickly. However, if such a scene were slowed down considerably, the images would hardly be able to scare you. In other words, visually triggered anxiety has an absolute weakness: it only works at speed. I would like to show you how the Slow Motion Technique exploits precisely this weakness to cancel fears within seconds, once again with the help of an example from my everyday work in my clinic.

A 27-year-old woman came to me in January 2015, suffering severe panic attacks and intrusive thoughts. Three years of therapy had not accomplished anything, and the antidepressants she had been taking for almost three years had only had one effect: making her gain over four stone. She told me that the panic attacks had started shortly after her 23rd birthday, when she wanted to take the metro in Berlin on her way to visit her boyfriend. Suddenly an image appeared in her head, a short sequence in which she could see how she threw herself in front of an approaching train and was crushed. She was quite startled and, from then on, was worried that this incident could repeat itself. The greater her fear was, the more frequently the image appeared in her head. Although she was in no way suicidal, in the coming weeks she avoided the metro and even taking any train at all, and later even the mere sight of railway tracks was enough to trigger a panic attack. The more she adopted avoidance behaviour, the greater the fear became that she might do something crazy to herself after all.

I asked her what exactly triggered her fear, and she said that it was always a fleeting image in her mind's eye: the scene in which she threw herself in front of the train. When I asked her if she had ever pictured the sequence slowly, in extreme slow motion, she looked at me in confusion and immediately said: 'Of course not, that would be horrible!' Then I asked her how she knew if it was truly horrible, because she had never tried it out after all. I said to her: 'Imagine that the moment you jump is so extended that you take ten minutes from the first muscle twitch to the moment you finally touch the tracks. After spending about five minutes in the air, moving towards the tracks, millimetre by millimetre. All the while, you have time to watch how the train also moves closer, millimetre by millimetre, while the face of the driver distorts in horror.'

I was able to observe how my patient followed my images and finally said with some disgust that that was silly, and of course it did not provoke any fear. At that point she had not yet understood that the same scene that had left her unable to take the metro for years was no longer any cause for fear as soon as she slowed it down enough.

Only gradually did she grasp that she herself had influence on whether the images in her head popped up suddenly or if she spent more time on them.

That very afternoon she descended the steps to the metro. Of course, the terrible image was present, but she forced herself not to repress it, but let it pass very slowly. That way she was actually able to remain standing and wait until the train approached. When the doors opened, she courageously boarded the train and she rode the four stops to her home for the first time in ages. She proudly trained this new behaviour every day. The unpleasant images came up every day at first. By the second week they only came up three times, and only once in the third week. The images had disappeared for ever by the fourth week because her brain had now learned that the flashing images of anxiety were no longer welcome.

In other words, a single session and a single technique was more effective than all those years of therapy and all the unnecessary medication. After that had been completely tapered off, losing weight was no longer a problem.

Most people believe they have to distract themselves as soon as anxiety washes over them, and unfortunately a significant number of therapists still consider this the correct and appropriate approach. However, the anxiety-triggering thoughts or images that are shooed off by distraction return. They come back again and again – in fact, as you read in Chapter 4.2.4., I compared it with a boomerang that slams into your head after you throw it away.

Once again, this fits quite well with my favourite quote from Albert Einstein, which I used at the start of this book: *'The definition of insanity is doing the same thing over and over and expecting different results.'*

So it is better to hold onto the negative thoughts and images and stay in control. You cannot be overcome by something that you have a firm grip on, and you can finally start to actively counteract it. As soon as you are able to change these images and thoughts in such a way that they no longer have a frightening effect, then it is just a matter of weeks until your brain has automated this new, pleasant behaviour.

Stop techniques for anxiety triggered by inner dialogues

Earlier in this chapter, you became familiar with the methods for putting a stop to the mental merry-go-round.

However, there are even more great techniques you can use to influence your inner dialogue so that the automatised processes of anxiety and panic and the related physical reactions can come to a stop.

The Auditory Slide Technique

Just like with the images, your inner dialogues, your thoughts, can be slid from one side to another. Just try it out! Take an anxiety-inducing sentence from your AUDITORY paper and pay attention to which side you can hear it more clearly. Then slide it from the negative ear to the positive. What change do you perceive first?

Can you tell how one and the same negative sentence, once shifted to the positive side, either cannot be heard at all, or is at least somehow off, distorted, or sounds unbelievable?

A significant number of my patients report that even the content of the words change as soon you just concentrate on the 'good ear'.

By the way, this technique also works exceptionally well with remembered conversations that we once had with someone else. A close acquaintance of mine said something very hurtful to me very long ago, and this had been seared into my memory for years. When I realised that I could only hear his words in my right ear, I repeatedly slid it to the left side and concentrated on only perceiving his voice in my left ear from then on. The voice immediately took on a more friendly tone in my head, and the words that were hurtful now felt completely different. I realised for the first time that he had only been giving me 'criticism' to protect me from something unpleasant. Since then, our relationship is significantly more relaxed and we have started seeing each other more frequently.

As already mentioned, the side that you hear negative things on does not necessarily have to be the same one where you see negative images. Around 2 per cent of people perceive negative images on the left side, but have the negative inner dialogues on the right side, or vice-versa. That is why you should try out for yourself what you perceive where, and slide it over to the other side.

My wife and I have now carried out this test with over 3,000 people and we are still astonished about the quick results we've seen, as well as the fact that this technique has not gained any currency in therapy circles. Only 7 per cent of my patients were unable or unwilling to use this technique, and the remaining 93 per cent immediately recognised its unbelievable potential and have used this method since then to have a better and anxiety-free life. However, for the remaining 7 per cent there is a technique that can be used, sooner or later, to overcome their fear – and this technique is even quite amusing.

The Pitching Technique

An additional, also very effective pattern breaker for auditory-triggered anxieties is the Pitching Technique.

Eight out of ten patients in my clinic have managed to use this technique to significantly reduce their anxiety immediately.

As with visually triggered fears, anxiety that is triggered by inner dialogues has an additional weakness in the area of speed. The word 'pitching' can mean 'tuning an instrument' or 'changing the level of pitch.' The sound of the voice changes when you make a recording go faster or slower. If the recording runs faster than normal, then the voice sounds higher and more frantic, but deeper and sluggish if the recording is slower.

When you think something, then you usually hear your own voice being spoken in your head. And because it is your voice, you basically trust what you are telling yourself. Would you have this same kind of trust if a high, squeaky voice was talking to you, or a very slow, deep monster voice? Probably not!

We only trust what we know. If we are unfamiliar with something, then we insert a critical judge between thinking and acting, and question the content of what we hear. Unfortunately, we do not automatically do that if we are hearing our own voice inside our heads. But that would be precisely the thing for anxiety patients to do in order to expose and disarm all their anxiety-inducing thoughts as quickly as possible. And this is where the Pitching Technique helps you.

As soon as you notice that you are causing anxiety with your thoughts, just imagine a small, ludicrous cartoon figure who says these thoughts for you. Although with this technique you will still hear negative sentences like: 'It's all too much, I'll never manage', you imagine them with a totally distorted pitch, for example a croaking, babbling animal voice like an excited Donald Duck, or the squeaky, theatrical voice of a Minnie Mouse.

This equally simple and often very amusing technique works so well because our brain is not able to perceive two contrary feelings at once. Either the inner dialogue causes anxiety because we hear it with our own voice, or it is absurd because a ridiculous little cartoon figure is desperately trying to scare us. At first, some – usually older – patients complain that it means they cannot take their fears seriously. However, anyone who has discovered this technique quickly understands that 'taking anxiety seriously' was precisely one of the main reasons why the anxiety disorder could spread the way it did.

Anxiety is like a small, stubborn child who furiously throws himself on the floor of a shop, screaming because he did not get any sweets. If you take this child's tantrum too seriously, then he learns that he can get his way by acting out, and you can bet that you will be seeing that behaviour frequently in the future. But if you ignore the child's defiant behaviour, it will soon be over, and then you will have a child who politely asks if he can have a sweet.

It is ultimately up to you to decide which technique you use to break through your anxiety. Some people love the Slide Technique and are fascinated with how the brain starts to automatically reformulate negative thoughts as positive ones; others find it easier to keep hold of the original thought, but make it absurd with the help of the Pitching Technique, so that the words can no longer deploy their negative energy. With a little practice, you can integrate all of these techniques into your daily life, and you will see that you are no longer helpless in the face of your anxiety-inducing thoughts.

Incidentally, many of my patients use the visual channel with the Pitching Technique. They imagine that the small, ridiculous cartoon character does not start to speak until it has jumped out of their head and started walking back and forth in front of them, gesticulating wildly. The more ridiculous the character is, and the funnier the voice sounds, the better the technique works. It is completely up to you whether you picture Mickey Mouse, a Smurf or the Minions. The less seriously you take the character, the better it is. The only thing that is important is that it says exactly the same thing to you that you would tell yourself as soon as your anxiety starts coming on. Remember, it is not about someone talking sense to you, but rather that you recognise how much you have been convincing yourself of your anxiety with your own thoughts. Although these are the same words, they no longer have any power over you as soon as you hear them in the voice of a Smurf or a Minion. Or would you really let something like that tell you how you should feel?

In psychology, this kind of transformative thinking is referred to as dissociation. Dissociating means you distance yourself from something in order to be able to examine it critically from a distance. This makes it much easier to check if what you are in the process of convincing yourself of is actually true, or if it just becomes 'true' by uncritically accepting it. Recently, a patient I had taught the Pitching Technique to came to their next session overjoyed, and showed me a Kinder Surprise toy. It was a small Smurf with a scythe, which was supposed to symbolise the patient's constant fear of death and illness. The patient told me that he had been carrying around it for days so that it reminded him to only hear his inner dialogue in the Smurf's voice. And in fact, every time he heard it he had to start grinning once he started projecting his negative thoughts onto this little blue squeaky-voiced Grim Reaper. The same thoughts that just weeks before had induced a shot of adrenaline now only made him chuckle.

Stop techniques for anxiety caused by physical sensations

In January 2014, a 72-year-old lady came to our clinic who in a telephone interview had told me she had a great fear of falling over. As soon as she entered the hallway, I noticed that she was searching for support from the wall. Once in the consulting room, she immediately reached for the back of the closest chair and gripped it frantically. When I asked her about it, she told me that she suffered from gait ataxia (permanent vertigo while walking, which appears frequently among the elderly). She said that she had gone from one doctor to the next for ten years without anyone being able to help her with her problem.

While she was standing I asked her to describe her vertigo more precisely. It was a rocking dizziness from left to right, as if she were walking on a ship being buffeted from the side by the waves. I asked her to imagine the vertigo was not going from left to right, but rather backward and forward. For a moment she had to focus entirely on how her body rocked back and forth. After a few seconds, I saw her starting to rock her upper body imperceptibly back and forth. Then I asked her to let go of the chair and take a few steps. After briefly hesitating, she did so and stopped in astonishment after a couple of steps, turned around, then took yet more steps, before finally looking at me in amazement. 'Mr Bernhardt, how is that possible? My vertigo is gone!' She took a few more steps, but her dizziness remained absent. I asked her to take a seat, and I could see that she could not believe what she had just experienced. So I explained to her what had happened in her brain during this short concentration exercise.

Neither the vertigo triggered by anxiety, nor the dizziness caused by gait ataxia, has anything to do with the vestibular system in the inner ear. Both forms of dizziness are purely and exclusively triggered by the brain – so you can turn it off there as well. If your brain makes you believe you are rocking from left to right, then you can give your brain a counter signal by imagining that you are rocking back and forth. Now your grey cells have a problem, because they cannot simultaneously carry out both signals, which is why they cancel each other out.

Such cancellation of contradictory impulses is nothing new and is well known in the field of physics. An acoustic wave can be completely dissipated by a counteracting sound wave, which can be created by frequency modulation. Motion can be stopped by counteracting motion. And with a little practice you can also stop the physical symptoms caused by the psyche, using conscious perception and corresponding counteraction.

My 72-year-old patient religiously practised the Counter Impulse after this session and the vertigo disappeared from her life. Her general health improved week by week because she was able to stop taking the medications she had been prescribed for her ataxia. When I bumped into her on the street three months later, she was laden down with shopping bags and she beamed at me. Now that she was able to walk around without any problem, she was catching up on everything she had missed out on.

The Counter Impulse

Unpleasant physical symptoms often have multiple levels where a Counter Impulse can be used. In addition to direction of movement, for example, there is temperature (hot or cold), weight (heavy or light), pressure (sharp or flat), flexibility (tense or loose) and possibly also colours (red or blue, for example) or brightness (bright or dark). Even if it may appear odd: the more details you can connect with your unpleasant feeling, the more Counter Impulses you can implement in a targeted way, and the easier it is for you to rid yourself of the symptoms – for ever. So, time to use your free lines on the KINAESTHETIC paper.

Here is a list of possible Counter Impulses that with a little practice you can use to cancel out the majority of physical symptoms triggered by anxiety.

DIZZINESS

- Cancel left/right dizziness with imagined dizziness back and forth.
- Cancel back/forth dizziness with imagined dizziness left to right.
- Cancel an anticlockwise spinning sensation with imagined clockwise dizziness.
- Cancel a clockwise spinning sensation with imagined anticlockwise dizziness.

THE SENSATION OF FALLING TO ONE SIDE

- Stop the feeling of falling forward with imagined falling backward.
- Stop the feeling of falling backward with imagined falling forward.
- Stop the feeling of falling to the left with imagined falling to the right.
- Stop the feeling of falling to the right with imagined falling to the left.

THE FEELING OF LOSING THE GROUND
BENEATH YOUR FEET

- If you have the feeling that the ground beneath your feet is giving way, picture the following: everywhere in the ground are hydraulic lifts. As soon as one of your feet touches the ground, they lift it up.

ITCHING IN ARMS AND LEGS

- Stop the 'ants' moving up your arm by imagining ants moving down your arm (or vice-versa).
- If the sensation is hot, then imagine it is ice cold.
- If you think of the colour red, then imagine the feeling is blue.

A SENSATION OF HEAT

- If you feel heat rising in your body, then imagine you are standing beneath an ice-cold shower and the water is flowing over your body and taking the heat with it.

It is not necessary to actually take a cold shower. After all, it is only a psychosomatically triggered sensation. Hard as it may be to believe, it is perfectly sufficient as far as your brain is concerned to merely take a cold shower in your imagination.

TIGHTNESS IN YOUR THROAT

- What does the tightness feel like exactly? Perhaps it can be compared with the feeling of wearing a collar that hangs heavy and warm around your neck? Then imagine that there is a cool, smooth stainless steel pipe in your throat that is slowly expanding and counteracting the collar: the first rips appear, the collar starts to split, then it falls off. End this exercise with several deep breaths, and visualise how easily the air is flowing through the smoothly polished, cool pipe.

TIGHTNESS IN YOUR CHEST

- Tightness in your chest is often described as a belt that someone has placed around your chest and pulled tight. Here, you can help yourself with the image that you have mechanical ribs of steel that you can use to expand your ribcage with the press of a button, meaning you can burst the belt whenever you feel like it, and you will be able to spread your lungs freely and with ease.

PRESSURE IN YOUR STOMACH

- Where do you sense the pressure coming from? Is it more of a sharp, stabbing pain from the outside to the inside, or is it the feeling that your whole stomach is contracting like a dark, cold lump? In the first case, imagine painful stabbing in reverse, so pressing from inside out. How does the pain change when you visualise this spike pressing from the inside out? You can dissolve the dark, cold lump by imagining your stomach is starting to illuminate, quickly spreading out through your belly and radiating a pleasant warmth.

These are only examples of what the irritating sensation might feel like. Please note exactly what your own physical symptoms feel like. Every detail that you can perceive and then change by imagining its opposite helps you to bring these sensations under control. Be prepared to experiment, and feel free to test which intense counter-feeling or counter-image produces the best result.

It is impossible to cause any harm with this exercise. After all, you only feel bad because of the way you have been thinking. So every effort to break through these old, unhealthy thought patterns can only do good, and will lead you step by step toward a life in which anxiety only arises when a real threat exists your body needs to warn you of.

It's important to remember to have patience. All these techniques are new for you, and you have to start by learning how to use them properly. The more frequently you counteract your problems, the faster you will be able to feel a difference, and the longer the desired effects will last. So please do practise this technique whenever you feel an unpleasant feeling come on, and do not be irritated when the fitting Counter Impulse seems nega-tive. Even a 'dark' or 'difficult' Counter Impulse has a positive effect if you identify the original negative feeling as 'bright' or 'light'.

You might be asking yourself why there are no Counter Impulses listed for problems with heart rate, breathing or swallowing, although these are very common symptoms for anxiety patients. Although I already tackled this issue in Chapter 5.1. I realise that many readers will start by jumping straight to the individual techniques instead of reading the book cover to cover, so I will briefly address the question here.

The heartbeat, breathing and swallowing are auto-matic from birth and work without our conscious effort. Humanity would surely be long extinct if these functions were dependent on our conscious brain.

In fact, exercises that place a focus on these three basic bodily functions can be harmful. The more you try to control a completely automated process, the greater the likelihood is that you will disturb it. You can picture it like clockwork in which every cog fits perfectly with the next. Everything is connected with everything else, and the second hand moves a small step forward every second. Do you think you can posi-tively influence the movement of this clock by trying to speed up and slow down one of the little wheels?

Probably not. It is more likely that you will cause it to stop working.

It is little different with your heartbeat, your breathing or the swallowing reflex. The sooner you are able to completely trust your body to control these processes all by itself, as is good and proper, the sooner you will be able to get rid of those unpleasant symptoms. Luckily, it is more than enough to regularly practise the 10 Sentence Method as well as the appropriate emergency techniques until your conscious mind quits wanting to control these automatic processes of its own accord.

But please bear in mind how long you might have trained your brain with 'false' thinking to generate not just anxiety, but also physical symptoms. Depending on the circumstances, it can take a couple of weeks until your focus is completely directed on your goals instead of your problems. Once you have succeeded at that, you will forget you ever wanted to monitor bodily functions that work perfectly quite automatically, and that is the way it should be.

Embodiment – a simple technique with powerful effects

We can see when someone is down, or angry, in love, or bone-tired. It is not just the facial expression, but also their posture that reveals how people feel. But does this mechanism work in reverse? Is it possible to produce a measurable influence on the psyche through a change in posture or facial expression?

In order to find out, in 1988, German psychologist Fritz Strack conceived an exciting experiment. He asked a group of people to read comics and then rate how funny they found them on a scale. A second group was also instructed to rate the comics, but they also had an additional task. While reading, they needed to clamp a pencil horizontally between their teeth. When the results were analysed, they determined that the subjects who chomped on the pencil found the comics much funnier than the control group. In the nineties, similar studies were conducted all over the world, and they all came to the same conclusion. The body is not only controlled by the psyche – even a consciously assumed posture can have a massive influence on your psychological state.

But what is behind the trick with the pencil? Try it out yourself. Put a pencil in your mouth and hold it horizontal with your teeth. If you look in a mirror, you will notice that your face automatically assumes a more positive expression. Of course, it is even better when you hold the pencil with your back teeth, which makes the effect even more pronounced than if you just used your incisors. As soon as you do this, the same muscles are tensed that you use to laugh.

Muscle memory now sends very specific information to your brain: 'I'm smiling, so I feel good!' But if you are not feeling great at that moment, your brain will bark back: 'Knock it off, I'm feeling horrible!' However, if you keep the pencil in your mouth, your muscle memory will continue to send the contradictory information. After about two minutes, your brain stops resisting and starts to conform its processing of the information to the constant firing of the muscles. After all, it has trained for a lifetime to bring body and soul into harmony.

In psychology, this phenomenon is called embodiment. Before you follow the impulse to swallow a sedative the next time you feel anxiety, try five minutes with a pencil. With a little patience, you can often achieve the same outcome, but without the side-effects.

The Power Pose

Amy Cuddy, the American social psychologist I mentioned in Chapter 2.5., activates the potential of embodiment by means of the Power Pose. The worse you are feeling psychologically, the more effective this method is. Here too, the idea is to adopt a pose that you would only assume when you are really feeling great. Cuddy also thought of taking blood from the participants directly before and after the Power Pose to see if their blood work reflected the positive effects. And indeed, she was able to prove that just changing posture was enough to reduce nearly all the relevant stress markers in the blood within minutes.

To assume the Power Pose Amy Cuddy used in her studies, just sit down in a comfortable chair, cross your arms behind your neck and put your feet up. You can use a table, a stool, or even another chair. The higher you put your feet, the more effective the pose is, so a table is definitely preferable to a low stool. Hold this pose for at least two or, even better, five minutes. Your testosterone levels climb appreciably during this period, and your cortisol levels sink. Because cortisol is the quintessential stress hormone, this exercise has a very immediate effect on your mood. It might seem hard to believe, but if you can hold this pose for five minutes, you will feel significantly better afterwards.

In order to actually be able to judge the positive effect, I also encourage my patients to write down – on a scale of one to ten – how anxious or depressed they feel before the exercise: 1 means negatives are almost imperceptible, while 10 stands for deeply despondent.

As soon as you relax from the Power Pose, you should examine your feelings again and note how much your psychological state has improved. Sometimes the feeling of anxiety or despondency will only fall from a 10 to 8 or 7, but the mood-boosting effect is usually much stronger.

Did you record the two numbers already? There you have it in black and white: you are no longer the helpless victim of your anxiety!

Summary:

- Fear is triggered mainly in the following three channels: the visual, the auditory and the kinaesthetic channel.
- Fear follows clear patterns that can easily be interrupted with some practice.
- Test all stopping techniques extensively and work with those that work well for you.
- Initially practise stop techniques in more harmless, negative situations, e.g. if you get irritated about your partner or child again. The better the techniques work here, the easier and safer you can use them in an impending panic attack.
- You will also find more information and detailed instructions on how to best use the stop techniques in the accompanying video course for this book, which can be found on my website: www.the-anxiety-cure.com.

6

FINALLY FREE FROM
ANXIETY AND PANIC
ATTACKS

Our brain saves everything that we perceive in the form of synaptic connections. Providing 'nourishment' for the brain is therefore of huge importance in getting and staying healthy.

If you have read and absorbed my book up to this point, then your brain has already undergone significant changes. Even thinking about this subject will have generated thousands upon thousands of new synapses, all primarily saving this one piece of information: change is possible and you too can achieve a happy and carefree life. If you have already begun the exercises, this effect will be much stronger, and I presume that you will have already enjoyed your first successes and are looking forward to your anxiety soon being over. Once you have reached your goal, there are still a few things you need to take into consideration if your success is to last.

Feeling great again! Now, how will you keep it that way?

All the techniques and exercises in this book are based on the latest neuroscience, which has shown beyond doubt that we can not only think ourselves sick, we can also think ourselves well. A decisive component of quick and lasting recovery is focus control. What you focus on will increase in your life. Concentrate on the successes you have already achieved and more will soon follow. But if you focus on the days when it 'still' is not going so well, then you will find yourself having more of those days as well.

Let's say that you have already managed to go a full week without panic and anxiety, followed by a small relapse. Whether you believe it or not, what you focus on now is what primarily decides what the next few weeks will be like. If you start thinking: 'There's no point, I'm still as sick as ever', your focus from then on will be on waiting for the next relapse, which becomes a self-fulfilling prophecy.

Instead, turn your attention to everything you have already succeeded in, for example, that you have spent an entire week free of anxiety for the first time in months or even years. Then, your unconscious will tell you: 'Wow, what a result. This is only a blip because I haven't finished rewiring my brain yet. I just need to keep going. If I can manage a whole week, then soon I'll be able to manage two or three – and then one day I'll have completely got over my anxiety.'

A happy and carefree life comes from a particular way of thinking. Since, regrettably, neither school nor society set particularly good examples for this way of thinking, you need to be self-sufficient in ensuring that your brain is exposed to enough positive examples. In some cases, that can mean reconsidering what sort of people you surround yourself with day in and day out. One of the most famous quotes from the American motivational speaker Jim Rohn goes: *'You are the average of the five people you spend the most time with.'*

Now don't worry, no one is asking you to kick your partner out of bed and pack your kids off to an orphanage. But it might make a lot of sense to ask yourself who these five people are, and whether they have just as much of a problem with change as you did until not so long ago. Or maybe you already have a relative or someone you know who has already managed to change their life. If it has been a long time since you have seen or spoken to this person, now is the time to get in touch with them again. Anyone who is equally as prepared as you to change their life for the better, and won't let themselves be discouraged by naggers, lazybones and naysayers from pursuing their dreams, is a better person for you to know than someone who whines year after year how hard and unjust everything is, but never does anything to change it. Everyone is master of their own destiny, and now that you also have the toolbox you need to get to work. Do it.

Stick at it! It's worth it!

I was fortunate to encounter the forerunner of today's 10 Sentence Method a decade ago while training in the United States. So impressed was I at its effectiveness that I decided to integrate it into my own life from that moment on. Since then I have been keeping a personal success diary, in which ten unfulfilled wishes are always written down. Three to four times a week I take a little time before I go to bed and work through one of these sentences in my thoughts, the way I described in Chapter 4.5. Once one of the wishes has become reality, I draw a smiley at the end of the sentence and begin thinking of a new one right away, so that I always have ten open wishes I can mentally work towards. In all these years not a month has gone by without at least one of the lines in my diary receiving a smiley face.

I have no doubt whatsoever that I would never have managed even 30 of these successes if I had not stuck conscientiously with the method. As it is, I can leaf through my success diary and take pride in the fact that I have achieved more than 100 goals already, all of which have made my life more pleasant, more exciting, more beautiful, or even simply more comfortable. In fairness, I also have to admit that some of the really big wishes stayed on that list for years on end and I had to work on them many times before I could finally tick them off with my smiley.

I often hear from acquaintances who I meet only every now and then remarks like: 'I can't believe everything you've done since we last met.' In contrast, I seldom hear the question: 'How on earth do you do it?' For those who still pose this question from time to time, I am happy to take them to one side and give them a detailed explanation of the secret behind my diary of success.

My advice for you is therefore: stick at it and keep your own personal success diary! Even once you feel on top of the world again, you should carry on with the 10 Sentence Method at least two or three times a week. My wife and I know of no better way to actively shape your life the way you want it. That is why we continue to use all the techniques described in this book.

Of course, you are perfectly free to use this programme for a happy and fulfilled life only when you feel really terrible. But if you do, please be aware that you are acting against your better judgement and quite possibly out of laziness to deny yourself all the unbelievable potential for growth that these techniques offer you.

Looking for advice, learning from experience

Just because a lot of people do things in a certain way is no guarantee that they are doing it the right way. I only seek advice on whether to do something or leave it from someone who is already where I want to be. So in future, think twice before you take advice from someone. Is this person living the life that you would like to lead? If not, you can stop listening to them, because they clearly do not know themselves what needs to be done. The experience of a good friend at a New Year's Eve party is an excellent example of this. He got chatting to a financial adviser, who at the end of a lively discussion asked if they could arrange a meeting. He had one or two ideas as to how my friend's savings could quickly be multiplied. Since the financial adviser seemed like a nice guy, my friend agreed, and they met a week later in a cafe.

While they were both waiting for their cappuccinos, my friend asked: 'Before we start, I have two important questions for you. First, how long have you been doing this, I mean, how much experience do you have?' Proudly, the financial adviser told him that he had been working in the branch for almost 20 years, naming two respected consultancy firms he had worked for, and boasted that he doubted there was anyone else in their region who knew the market as well as he did.

'That's terrific,' my friend said, delighted, and posed his second question: 'How many millions do you have in the bank?' His interlocutor stared at him in bafflement and said: 'This isn't about me, we're meeting today because you want to get a return on your money.' To which my friend replied: 'No, no, don't get me wrong. If you're as good as you say you are, and you've been doing this job for almost 20 years, then in all that time you must have earned a small fortune and made it even bigger with your investments. If you haven't, then you clearly don't know what you're doing, in which case you're definitely not someone I need to take financial advice from.' It goes without saying that this meeting did not last very long.

If you take advice from someone, whether that is about money, where to go on holiday or about your health, you should only listen to people who know what they are talking about and can point to their achievements to prove it.

Why aren't more therapists using these methods?

One of the commonest reactions I hear in my clinic is: 'This is incredible, these techniques work so fast. Why aren't many more therapists using these methods?'

That is a very good question. I am certain that there are no doctors or therapists who would intentionally refuse to help you. Each of them will try to help you as best they can based on what they know. Sadly, what they know is often 12 to 15 years out of date. Yet this is not something that one ought to hold against the profession, for there is a very simple, rational explanation for it.

When scientific research delivers new insights, they must be published in a specialist journal so that fellow experts in the field can discuss the findings and conduct further tests. The most important of these journals are *Science* and *Nature*, and being published in one of the two is crucial to receiving worldwide attention and the likelihood of further investigation. The demand to be published in them is high. It usually takes one to two years for an article to go through all the phases of criticism and revision before finally achieving the high standard these journals demand.

Once the article has finally been published, different researchers will start investigating the findings, conduct their own studies, and even attempt to disprove the new claim if it goes against commonly held beliefs.

Somewhere around three to five years later a consensus starts to form around this new knowledge, and, with a little luck, by general agreement it will be considered 'recognised'. Only now will the new information finally find its way to specialist publishers and into the textbooks that will be used to teach future generations of doctors and therapists. Yet this process too takes time; after all, teaching materials need to be created, edited and accepted into the syllabus.

This is the work of months, or even years if the new approach diverges strongly from the previously accepted wisdom. Only once this is complete can new curricula be drawn up, another long-term process.

Once the new course materials are finally available, those cutting-edge insights will already be somewhere between five and eight years old. Unfortunately, neither universities nor students can afford brand-new teaching materials in every subject every year.

Depending on the financial situation of the university, here too a considerable amount of time might pass before prospective doctors and therapists get their hands on an up-to-date textbook. When they have finally finished studying five years later and get to treat their first patient, the majority of what they know is already 12 to 15 years old.

So as you can see, no one is spreading obsolete science on purpose. Rather, we are dealing with perfectly normal development and training cycles, whose significance however remains a mystery to many.

Before I became a therapist myself I spent almost 20 years working as a TV journalist covering science and medicine. Through my job I had the great good fortune to learn about new approaches in therapy very early on. Since I was also closely acquainted with people who had been suffering for years with a variety of anxiety disorders, I always had a very good overview of the different types of therapy that were already on offer and those that anxiety patients might have to wait years for. It is thanks to the happy circumstance of my prior career path that I was one of the first people in Europe to put all these fantastic new techniques into practice, and even develop them further in my clinic. So please have some understanding if your previous therapist or psychiatrist has not heard anything about these techniques – yet.

Pick the right motivational strategy!

I owe much to one of my early coaches, who coined the following striking phrase: *'People change for one of two reasons: big failures or big dreams!'*

When you think it over, you will realise that you too have been drawing all your power to change from one of these two sources. Only when you wanted something so much that you were prepared to do anything for it, or when a situation was so awful that you did not want to put up with it a second longer, were you prepared to make change happen.

Sadly, anxiety patients tend to be exceptionally good at bearing the unbearable until the pain overwhelms them. What they have forgotten over the years is the capacity to set themselves new and better goals and use these targets to give themselves the strength of mind necessary to achieve them step by step.

So start dreaming again, for example, how it might be to finally have a career that is also a calling. Something that you enjoy doing so much it does not feel like work any more. It might be hard to believe right now, but there is a job like that out there for you, and it is quite possible that one day you will earn your living doing it. I can say this with such certainty because I have already accompanied many of my patients on this very road, and I still do on a regular basis within the framework of my workshops.

By the way, it is completely okay if this new calling does not come to you unprompted. How could it? After all, for years your brain has been trained to see only problems. You will need to learn to think in terms of solutions again. One major problem is that so many people still believe that they need to set 'realistic' goals. They avoid setting big targets for fear of disappointment if they do not come up to scratch. What they are overlooking is that it is those 'unrealistic' goals themselves that unleash inside them the necessary strength and desire to start taking action.

Here, we are dealing with a problem common to many people and especially anxiety sufferers. Imagine there are 100 people who all have the same big dream. Yet to this day 97 of them have not managed to make it a reality, even though they have been dreaming about it for many years. What do you think would be the clever thing to do? Join up with the 97 and echo them: 'Yeah, it's really not that simple, so many people have tried it but it hardly ever seems to work?'

Do you really believe that brings you any closer to your goal? Or would you go to the other three, who actually managed to do it, and would you ask them if they would kindly share what they did differently that made it possible to live the dream? Maybe you will learn a thing or two that might just bring you a decisive step in the right direction.

Final thoughts

A couple of years ago I was asked during a radio interview if I was able to sum up the core message of my therapy work in one or two sentences. The spontaneous response I gave is now the guiding principle of my work, and not a day goes by in my clinic in which I don't give one of my patients this piece of advice:

> You don't have to be healthy to live your dream life. You can start living your dream life, so you can finally be healthy!

It is my heartfelt wish that you too, dear reader, will step by step be able to find your way back to a life full of lightness and joy. If this book helped you on your way there, then it would of course be a great pleasure for me if you would pass the recommendation on. Especially for anxiety sufferers, the experiences of people who have been in the same situation are a crucial factor in deciding to try this new form of therapy.

It all begins with questioning your own thought processes and then, invigorated by the first successes of a new way of thinking, tackling the – perhaps long overdue – changes that need to be made, bit by bit.

If you know of other methods that you have had good experiences of with combatting anxiety, I would love to hear from you. I am constantly on the lookout for new knowledge that helps anxiety patients get a joyful life back more quickly and easily, and if you know of anything that could help me, please share it with me at: Bernhardt@Panikattacken-loswerden.de

Many thanks!

STAY INFORMED

If you wish to find out more about the latest scientific findings regarding anxiety, panic disorders and happiness, then please register for our free newsletter on our website.

I have also put together a list of fantastic books and audiobooks on our website, www.the-anxiety-cure.com. Whether you want to discover new ways of thinking, or need support changing jobs, in your relationship or your social life, the books I recommend are packed with valuable tips, and more than one of these books has brought me a giant step forward on my own path. Always remember that you alone are responsible for the information you provide for your brain every day, and you will only get good results with good raw materials.

Some of my book tips:

Medical advice
Kelly Brogan, MD *A Mind of Your Own: The Truth About Depression and How Women Can Heal Their Bodies to Reclaim Their Lives*

How our brain works
Dr Julia Shaw *The Memory Illusion*
Daniel Kahneman *Thinking, Fast and Slow*
Dan Ariely *Predictably Irrational. The Hidden Forces That Shape Our Decisions*

Life coaching
Richard Wiseman *59 Seconds: Change Your Life in Under a Minute*
Richard Wiseman *Rip It Up: The Radically New Approach to Changing Your Life*
Byron Katie *Loving What Is: Four Questions That Can Change Your Life*

Good for business
Stephen R. Covey *The 7 Habits of Highly Effective People*
Tim Ferriss *The 4-Hour Workweek*

Relationship advice
Dale Carnegie *How To Win Friends & Influence People*
Enjoy reading!

Yours
Klaus Bernhardt

ACKNOWLEDGEMENTS

This book would never have been possible without the help of many wonderful people. I would particularly like to thank my beloved wife Daniela, who together with me runs our Berlin clinic. She gave me the space I needed, evening after evening and weekend after weekend, to make sure this book was ready on schedule. She is also a fantastic therapist in her own right, whose professional expertise proves immeasurably valuable for me again and again.

I would also like to thank the entire team at Ariston Verlag as well as my agent Lars-Schutze Kossack and his wife Nadja. They all provided invaluable support in making my work available to the widest audience possible. As a result, not just anxiety patients but ever more therapists have been exploring our work.

In this respect, I would particularly like to thank all the colleagues who have already contacted us. It is thanks to your interest that we have been able to start offering training courses in order to make this new form of therapy as widely available as possible. Especially gratifying in this regard is that ever more doctors and psychotherapists are taking an interest in our approach, and are prepared to cross the aisle to talk to us. It is precisely this open exchange that we need so that together we can continue to develop better therapy methods for the benefit of all anxiety patients.

REFERENCES

1. Roemheld syndrome: When gas leads to fear
   H. Emminger, T. Kia (Ed.) *Exaplan: Das Kompendium der klinischen Medizin,* 7th edition, Elsevier, Urban & Fischer 2011, p. 23

2. The biological storage of thoughts
   Prof. Dr. E. Kandel *Auf der Suche nach dem Gedächtnis: Die Entstehung einer neuen Wissenschaft des Geistes,* Pantheon 2007

3. White coat syndrome: When anxiety raises blood pressure
   T. V. Khan, S. S. Khan, A. Akhondi, T. W. Khan White coat hypertension: relevance to clinical and emergency services personnel, in *MedGenMed*, p. 52, Review PMID 17435652, 13 March 2007

4. The effect of posture on the psyche
   D. Carney, A. J. C. Cuddy, A. Yap Power posing: Brief non-verbal displays affect neuroendocrine levels and risk tolerance, in *Psychological Science*, 21, pp. 1363–1368, 2010

5. Meta-analysis by Jay Fournier on the effectiveness of antidepressants
   J. Fournier et al. Antidepressant Drug Effects and Depression Severity: A Patient-Level Meta-Analysis,

in JAMA (*Journal of the American Medical Association*), pp. 47–53, 6 January 2010

6. Countering the false thoughts that we accept
B. Katie *Loving What Is*, Rider, 2002

7. How specific use alters the brain
K. Woollett, E. A. Maguire Acquiring 'The Knowledge' of London's Layout Drives Structural Brain Changes, in *Current Biology*, Vol. 21, Issue 24, pp. 2109–2114, 8 December 2010

KLAUS BERNHARDT worked for years as a science and medical journalist before two of his friends started to suffer from anxiety and asked him for help. He immersed himself in anxiety research, trained to become a complementary psychotherapist and developed his own treatment methods with staggering success rates. Klaus Bernhardt runs a psychotherapy clinic in Berlin that specialises in treating anxiety disorders, and is a member of the Akademie für neurowissenschaftliches Bildungsmanagement (AFNB) and the Initiative Neues Lernen e.V. (INL).

www.the-anxiety-cure.com

INDEX